THE LONG CAMINO

JT Diaz

Halo
PUBLISHING
INTERNATIONAL

ISBN: 978-1-63765-172-8
LCCN: 2022901493

Halo Publishing International, LLC
www.halopublishing.com

Printed and bound in the United States of America

For Papi (Gabriel Diaz)

Contents

Chapter 1

Single Mother

"Let's go, keep the line moving!" is all they keep hearing from the raspy voice of an officer who has the stench of cigarettes and old coffee. It is a hot day in El Paso, Texas. The line of people who have been traveling for weeks without a bath or doing laundry has caused a pungent smell even in the outdoor area. Many of the travelers are only wearing one set of clothes, while a few limp due to lost shoes that caused worn-out socks and bleeding blisters. Some take cardboard or any trash that can be found to make a shoe and wrap it with tape or clothing in hopes that it will last until their destination. Exhausted, hungry, and in pain, they all seem to have different looks about them. Several of them have a confused, blank stare, unsure of what is happening or where they were. Others are upset because they have been here before and know the process. A few, happy because they feel that they made it to where they needed to be.

"Come on, get in, and find a seat," the travelers are told as they make their way onto the bus. It is difficult to walk with the cold steel gripped tightly around their ankles and the chains that barely extend enough to make a full step. The sound of the metal scraping along the floor and hitting the seat legs, along with the officer's commands, is all that Joaquin can hear.

Joaquin slowly makes his way down that narrow aisle of the bus. The much younger travelers are patient and help him if they see him struggling too much. It is even more difficult for Joaquin due to his having a sharp pain running down his leg; it started in his lower back. He still manages. This is not Joaquin's first ride on these buses. Though, with his age and all that he has gone through, he feels this may be his last trip. Joaquin takes his seat and attempts to make himself comfortable. It proves to be a bit difficult with the chains around his waist pinching the skin at his belly. The digging into his back from the chains and the angle that the restraints are around his wrist make it uncomfortable.

He was only along for the ride to another facility where he will have to take another bus and be put on a plane to Honduras. Everyone on the current bus, from what he can see, has just made their way from Ecuador, El Salvador, and Honduras. He even hears some Portuguese being spoken, so he assumes some are from Brazil. The facility he just departed from had people from all over the world.

Joaquin sits there, gazing out the window as the bus makes its way through the many gated doors, each time having to stop as an officer checks, with a rolling mirror, to see if anything or anyone is underneath the bus somehow.

Then, losing himself in thought, Joaquin can only think about how he got here after so many years.

It was a cool evening for this time of year in Honduras. The year was 1955 and *La Semana Santa* was just underway. Clear evening skies gave the moon an opportunity to light up the normally dark pathways throughout the little village of Valle de Angeles. Villagers filled the streets and pathways as the roads were blanketed with bright colors, and paintings of Biblical figures can be found everywhere. People were all dressed up, paying tribute to the upcoming Easter holiday only a week away. Everyone seemed to be happy and positive, despite everything that was going on.

Honduras was going through big changes with the Communist party taking over, and that caused this small country to be divided. Roads were unsafe due to a group called the RCH (Republic Communist of Honduras) patrolling and pressuring citizens of the country to turn to the party freely or it will be forced upon them. Most of the villagers were able to steer clear of these roadblocks, knowing the land and having their own routes. No one knew what was to become of the country, but one thing was certain Joaquin Tejirina Navarez was on his way. With Tegucigalpa six hours away on foot, it was the closest big city, and there was no way a hospital would be within reach for this couple expecting their third child.

The loud cries from little Joaquin is all you could hear throughout the quiet village as his parents hugged and kissed one another. Joaquin's mother was exhausted, and she was sweating from all the work she put in to deliver him. *La partera* (midwife) was no stranger to this couple. She had delivered their previous two children, and she had given help to many of the expecting mothers within the village. She wrapped the newly born child and gave him to the exhausted mother. All were happy at the sight of a perfect, healthy child as he lay on the chest of his mother. Joaquin's mother just stared at him with the eyes only a mother can give to her child. His father was happy, and he was gently touching Joaquin's head as *la partera* finished cleaning things up. She was thanked for all she had done, but quickly left because she needed to make her way to another home, as there was another child being born that evening.

In the home where a young couple was expecting their first child, *la partera* entered, ready to begin delivering the baby. The entire family had gathered around, anxious for the coming of the little child. Only her mother and sister, along with her husband, were in the room. All the rest of the family had to wait in the living area. The expecting mother was in a great deal of pain as the baby was moving and preparing its arrival into this world. As the midwife warmed up the water and gathered blankets and towels, she heard a loud bang at the door. Smoke filled the room from the blast, and shards of glass were thrown everywhere, breaking against the walls and floor.

Several men entered the room, headed towards the husband of the young, expecting couple. This young man was working at the banana factory (as do most men, since there isn't much work), and it was rumored that he was speaking against the RCH and trying to aid those who opposed the

Communist regime. *"¡¡¡TÍRATE AL SUELO!!!"* Get on the floor, they demanded.

The young couple looked on with terror as the men entering the home grabbed all those in their path and tossed them to the floor. Once the men reached the couple, one of the men grabbed the husband by his hair and throat. No expression at all in his face, the man simply held the young husband, who was screaming and demanding to be released. *"¡¡¡¡DÉJAME IR!!!!"*

Another man, with the same inexpressive face, grabbed the wife, who was on the bed. In so much pain with the baby coming, she was helpless as the man dragged her off the bed. He grabbed her by the hair and pulled violently as her body hit the floor. She began kicking and screaming, as well as trying to hold her stomach to protect her baby. Cries and screaming, from both the family in the house and the intruders, filled the room.

"It has come to our attention that you have aided the other party in hopes to remove us from power," the assailant that held the young husband by the hair and throat began. "We have come to show you, and the others you work with, that we are here and will not go anywhere. You will all surrender and follow what we have demanded or face the consequences of your actions."

The young, expecting mother is still holding her stomach, crying in pain as the baby isn't waiting. The midwife pleads to tend to the mother, but is quickly quieted by another man who strikes her in the face with the butt of his rifle. Fear grows in the eyes of the expectant mother as she witnesses la partera lying there motionless, blood flowing from the large gash opened up below her eye and nose.

The pain was too unbearable, and she curled up holding her stomach. The man still firmly grasping her hair yanked hard and told her to be quiet, but as the baby was making its way, she could not hold back the screaming pains of childbirth. The first man, holding her husband, turned and demanded his partner shut her up. So, the man holding the wife drew out a large knife and began slowly slicing her stomach back and forth several times. The first entry produced shock, as the expectant mother was not expecting such barbaric treatment. Those that followed after quieted the mother out of despair and disbelief that this was actually happening.

Once the man stopped with his knife, the expectant mother no longer felt the movement of the baby. The wounds to her stomach had not even hurt, compared to the pain of when the child was coming, so it was as if she felt nothing at the moment. With a feeling of defeat, the expectant mother stopped resisting and just let her body fall. Holding her stomach, she began to cry even louder than when she was in pain.

The man, who grabbed her hair once again, found a place for his knife. He pulled her head up, exposing her neck; then, with the already bloodied blade, he ran it across her throat from left to right.

The young husband looked on with disbelief as his mutilated wife dropped to the floor with a loud thud. Blood pouring from her stomach and throat was what he saw as his wife choked on her own blood and became lifeless. The image before him became blurred as tears filled his eyes, and any sound became muffled around him at the sight of his wife and child now gone. The man holding him let him go, and he quickly ran to his wife.

As the young husband grabbed his wife, the man who had been holding him reached for his gun, pointed it at the back of his head, and fired. He then pulled a handkerchief from his breast pocket and wiped a speckle of blood that had gotten on the barrel of the gun. Signaling for the other men to leave the home, on his way out he said, "You will learn to live with us and our ways or more will happen."

Down the way in Joaquin's home, his parents heard the loud explosion, and they quickly gathered some items. It had been told that these raids were happening throughout the country, and it was getting closer to them. They just were unsure how much time they had before it reached them. There was a second explosion.

The invading men had a list of people whom they were told to find and "interrogate." Their interrogation methods were quickly seen, and the whole village was shaken. Their orders were simple—find these men, and eliminate them and their families as a warning to those who oppose them. The villagers had no way of defending themselves against this group of men.

After gathering some things, Joaquin's parents fled into the woods and headed towards the mountains. Joaquin's father knew they would be coming for him next, so he had to save his family. They ran through most of the night until they could no longer continue. His mother had to make several stops due to still recovering from childbirth. Joaquin's mother and two older brothers took turns holding Joaquin as they made their way through the darkness of the jungle. They were about ten and twelve years old as Joaquin's brothers traded off carrying their little brother.

It seemed as if a lifetime had passed since they began running; they could no longer go on. Joaquin's mother needed to rest as she had blood running down her legs from where she was still unhealed. The lack of oxygen and loss of blood had caused her to become very pale, and her muscles started cramping. Her husband decided to find a safe place to hide for the night. For fear of being found, they did not light a fire and found a small rock formation that would give them some cover. The boys fell asleep quickly. Their father stayed awake as long as he could, making sure that they were not followed.

It was the sound of dogs that woke her. Joaquin's mother awoke and felt the stiffness in her muscles, but that quickly subsided as panic crept in, and she began to move quickly. She looked around and could not see her husband and two other boys. She peeked over the rocks to try and see them, but could not from where she was. As the dogs seemed to be getting closer, she didn't know what to do since her family was nowhere in sight. She held on to Joaquin and began to run, trying to stay out of sight. Her running quickened as she felt someone coming from behind her. It was her husband, alone.

"*¿Dónde están los niños?*" Where are the children, she pleaded.

He simply held a finger to his mouth to quiet her down because the men and those dogs were very close. He led her quietly to where the boys had been near the creek. The dogs started barking loudly as they pointed in the same direction as where the boys were. The men released the dogs as they darted towards the direction of the two boys. Their parents tried to get there, and the husband left his wife to try and save the boys.

Joaquin's mother looked on with horror as the first dog tackled the younger son and started biting at his arms and swinging him from side to side in the air like a doll. The other two dogs joined in, and all three of them viciously attacked the ten-year-old boy. Their teeth sank into the soft skin of his face and chest, and his crying was stopped as one grabbed him by the throat and shook his head from side to side violently. The older boy kept running, making it to his father, but was met with several men surrounding them. The dogs were called off, and with their blood-soaked fur, they joined their masters and sat at their feet, waiting for their next command.

The older boy cried with fear, and the father tried to comfort him even though he knew what was going to happen. He told his son that everything was going to be all right and that he had nothing—

The crack of a gun stopped the father from finishing his sentence, and he felt the burning of something in his stomach. Then another and another. The shots he kept hearing would find their way into his older son and then into his own body. As he looked down into his son's eyes, they glazed over and rolled back. He set his son down, as if laying him on a bed, and tried to get up, but was met with more bullets. The father fell hunched over on his son.

Joaquin's mother could see only when her husband fell onto her son and knew they were gone. As she lay there hidden and unable to move for fear of being found, she held the little baby close, having latched him on to her breast so that he did not make any noise. She simply gazed at her family, torn to shreds and mowed down by bullets. The men looked around to be sure there was no other movement and, content with what they did, left.

For what seemed like many hours, Joaquin's mother stayed in that spot until it started to become nightfall. She then came out from her spot of hiding and went to her family. The younger son was unrecognizable, and the other two lay together in a pool of their blood. She had nowhere to go and no one to turn to. The only thing that she thought of was to head north. Head as far north as she could, until the smell of her family's blood was no longer in the air. Far enough north so that these men could not find her and finish what they started. She knew that the only place she could go was *los Estados Unidos*.

Chapter 2

Deceived

Back on the bus, Joaquin felt his hand going numb, so he tried to adjust the metal restraint he had on. It may have been a little too tight as it was leaving deep red indents on his skin. He brushed it off, thinking to himself, *They've been a lot tighter.* He began trying to remember some of his earliest memories as a child growing up. Though, it was pretty difficult since he was getting up there in years. He recalled when he was old enough to remember asking his mother about his father. It always brought her to tears, but she would tell Joaquin that his father was the bravest and strongest man she had ever known. He always stood up for what was right and would do anything to protect and save his family.

They didn't make it to *los Estados Unidos* as his mother had planned. They couldn't even make it out of Honduras. The PCH had the border well guarded, and all those who attempted to leave were shot. There were stories of how some would make it through the barrier of men, only to be caught in Guatemala. The PCH had men everywhere and would catch those who escaped and drag them back behind their horses or motorcycles. The bodies were tied by their hands or feet while they were mostly still alive. The long, rocky road that they were dragged on would peel off their skin. Many feared to be caught, so they didn't try to flee.

Joaquin and his mother stayed where they could, and most people would help her since she had a baby with her. She was still determined to get away from Honduras, to a better place for her son. However, going right then, with Joaquin a newborn, was dangerous, and she did not want to take the chance of losing him as well.

Joaquin and his mother found a place to stay for a while at her cousin's house; they were away working the fields. He was called to by his mother, "¡Ven aquí!" Come here, she called.

Joaquin knew it was close to dinnertime, but he had to fight off the last of the "bad men," as his father had done. His imagination took him everywhere, and today was no exception. He had his stick, and, swinging it around like a sword, he would hit a tree, pretending it was "bad men." Swing after swing, the sword would find its mark, slicing easily through the flesh of the men. It was like a warm knife through butter; Joaquin was able to cut through the clothes and body armor of the men who had taken his father and two brothers. "I'm coming, Madre," he yelled back before ripping the head off his last assailant. Cleaning the sword on his arm, he felt victorious and content with his work. As he sheathed his sword, he walked back towards the house with his head held high.

"Be sure to wash up. I don't want you tracking dirt in here, *sucio*!" his mother shouted at him.

Covered in the blood of his enemies, Joaquin ran to the water spout and used the hose that leaked from all the cracks in it due to its sitting out in the hot sun. As he washed away the dirt from his hands and face, he knew he did a good job protecting his mother today.

"How many did you get today, *mijo*?" his mother asked.

"I only got four today," he said with a long, sad face as he dragged his feet on the floor and found his place at the table.

"The bad men must have been hearing of the great warrior that is killing them, and so they must be scared to come now," his mother said with an encouraging tone.

This brought a smile on his face, and he jumped off his seat and ran to his mother, who was still cooking, and gave her a giant hug. After he slowly let her go, he grabbed a piece of the meat she had next to her and ran off.

With the spatula in her hand, she quickly smacked his hand as he laughed and ran. "¡*Ay, niño loco!* Get out of here before I show you how good I am with a sword!"

That evening a knock at the door startled them both, as they hadn't been expecting anyone. It was a friend of hers, and his mother told Joaquin to please go to the other room. He couldn't hear completely what they were discussing, but it must have been something good because his mother was happy. "*Vámanos*, let's go. We must hurry and pack some things," his mother said with a sense of urgency.

With a confused look on his face and uncertain why, he began to grab the few little things he had with him. "What's going on, Mama? Why are we packing?" he asked a couple of times before she answered.

"Remember when I would tell you that one day we would go to America and be free from all the bad men? Well, tonight we have the opportunity to make that happen. We must hurry though, or we'll miss the truck."

Joaquin's mother would always tell him that America was the best place to be—"*la tierra de la libertad*," as she would call it—the land of the free. "We can go and be what we want and do what we want, and no one can tell us otherwise."

The thought of doing what he wanted and being whatever he wanted was more than enough of a reason for Joaquin to go. He grabbed what he could and stuffed it into a bag that his mother gave him. His mother finally finished gathering her items, put out the fire, and let the goat go free. She was not expecting to come back and didn't want the goat to starve. When they both were ready to leave, they headed for the road to where the truck was waiting.

Joaquin was excited and nervous at the same time. He was going to a new country, and they wouldn't have to worry about fighting "bad men" anymore. He thought about the different places he could go and all the different adventures he could go on. His mind was racing a million miles an hour. "I wonder if they'll have *macheteadas* there. That's my favorite in the morning." As he thought about everything that he hoped would be at their new home, he remembered something he had forgotten. "Oh no, Papi's pocketknife!" He and his mother were already on the road when Joaquin remembered his father's pocketknife that his mother had given him. It was a simple knife that had a white handle with a carving in it that didn't look like anything. Joaquin told his mother that he thought that the handle looked like a bone to him. She had told him that the knife was passed down from his father and his father before him.

His mother was in such a hurry because she didn't want to miss the truck. She yelled at Joaquin, "*¡Solo déjalo!* Just leave it. We don't have time. We must keep going!"

Joaquin didn't want to leave without the only thing that linked him to generations of Navarezes. He ran back to the house, where he knew the knife would be. The knife wasn't there. Joaquin's mother was yelling at him to get back because they had to leave. He was determined to get his father's knife despite his mother's pleading.

It was then that she heard the all-too-familiar sound. The howling of the dogs in the distance. Fear swept over her immediately. It seemed as though it were just yesterday that she watched as her ten-year-old was being shredded by the dogs and torn beyond recognition. Now, again she dreaded the same thing happening as the dogs were getting closer and her son was not in sight.

Joaquin's head jumped up at the sound of the dogs, and panic hit him. He remembered where he put the knife. He used it earlier to cut some fishing line near the bathroom. He was trying to clean some fish he caught at a nearby creek.

He grabbed the knife and ran for his mother, who was anxiously waiting at the road.

"Don't you ever do that again! Do you hear me? ¿¿Me oyes?? You can't leave my sight anymore until we get to America. We must go now!" she yelled frantically at Joaquin.

The sound of the dogs was getting closer and closer. Joaquin and his mother didn't stop running. As they were getting closer to the place she was supposed to meet the truck, she noticed a few others running as well.

"¡Vámanos! Hurry! We have to hurry! They know about the truck!" a man was yelling towards everyone who was running.

She saw the truck in sight after about five minutes of running and noticed many other people around the truck, trying to get on. The dogs seemed very close, and the cracking of their barks sent chills down Joaquin's mother's spine. Then her heart sank as she noticed the truck start moving. Many of the people were still trying to get on, and she and Joaquin still hadn't made it there. She ran, pulling Joaquin, and he missed a few steps, but was able to keep up as much as he could. She was able to reach the truck in time, just as she saw the men and the dogs. She couldn't tell if they were the same ones, but she knew they had to get on that truck. There were others still running from the woods, also trying to get on the truck, but they were met with a spray of bullets that stopped their attempts at escape.

With help from some of the men, his mother was able to get herself and Joaquin on the moving truck. As she sat and held Joaquin tightly, one of the men said, "It's going to be okay; we made it." Just as he finished his sentence, Joaquin's mother closed her eyes in disbelief that they were able to escape. She then felt something wet hit her face. When she opened her eyes again, the man who had been speaking had a bullet hole in his head, and she realized it was his blood and brain matter that had hit her in the face. More bullets followed, and those who were standing or closest to the door of the truck met the same fate. As the truck picked up speed, the sounds of the dogs grew more distant, and the bullets that hit the truck sounded like hail hitting tin. Eventually, that stopped as they were too far away.

The truck that they were on had a driver that used to be with PCH, and he knew of routes that he could take and get people to safety or out of the country. He had left PCH after realizing that he didn't want to be killing his countrymen. When the PCH found out that he had turned on them, they sought him out, killing all the people to whom he was related. They would take the men and tie their hands to a tree and their feet to cattle; then, with a hot iron, they would poke the cattle, causing them to run forward, dismembering the men. The cattle would drag the half-torn men through the village. Then, with the women, they would have their way with them, each taking turns, and when they finished, they would line them all up, shoot them, and then hang them in the trees as a display for all to see. As for the children, they would bind their hands and feet with a rope attached to a large stone and toss them into the river. Knowing this, no one wanted to turn on the PCH for fear of this happening to his or her family. The driver knew his time was limited, and since his family was all gone, he wanted to help as many as he could before he was caught and killed.

Once they were a safe distance away, he pulled over, and they removed the bodies of those who had been killed. He secured the back door and locked it from the outside. It was a small shipping-container-type truck bed, so there were no windows and no air movement, just a small opening at the top for a vent. They were given a few buckets and some old newspapers, in case they needed to use the restroom, along with some flashlights and blankets. It was going to be a long ride, and they would stop for food when they could.

Once the truck was moving again, Joaquin was holding on to his mother tightly. "I'm sorry, Mommy!" he began saying apologetically. "I won't ever do that again."

"It's okay, *mijo*, we're safe now, and that's all that matters. Soon we will be in America, and all will be fine. Just you wait and see," his mother said while tears swelled in her eyes.

Since there were no windows on the truck, the people couldn't tell what time of the day it was. The hole at the top of the truck didn't show much light because it was slightly covered so no rain would come in. The heat inside was astounding. Temperatures reaching in the one hundred twenties was not something the people inside wanted to go through. With that heat it caused the buckets of human waste to smell even more, and most of the people hadn't bathed in a few days. A few times they hit big bumps, which caused the buckets to spill over. There was nothing they could do to stop from getting covered in urine and feces. It was starting to become unbearable for some, and agitation started growing amongst some of the men. The look on some of the villagers' faces showed growing uneasiness; they seemed be wondering if it was the right decision to leave or if it would have been better to stay in Honduras. Either way, there was no going back now, and they had to face together what was to come on this road.

At the start of this trip, there was a younger mother with a baby who wouldn't stop crying. After a couple of days, the crying stopped. The air inside got thicker and thicker, making it difficult to breathe. An older lady who was sitting next to Joaquin and his mother had given them a better space for them to sit. She was pretty talkative from what Joaquin could remember. *"Me llamo Anita. ¿Cómo estás?"* she said to Joaquin's mother.

"Hola, me llamo Gloria, and this is Joaquin," his mother responded. The conversation took off, and Joaquin lost interest, being that it was adults talking and that he was very tired. The last thing he heard before falling asleep was his mother telling Anita about how she lost her husband and two older sons.

He was awakened by how hot it was and how difficult it was to breathe. He noticed his mother sleeping. So was Anita; her sleep was different though. He couldn't see her breathing, and, like everyone else, she wasn't sweating. He thought nothing of it, so he just adjusted himself and tried to go back to sleep.

The truck finally came to a stop after what seemed like three days. They had stopped before, but only to fuel up or to empty the buckets and hand out water and sandwiches. The banging on the door woke Joaquin and his mother. She quickly got up and gathered her things. She called out to Anita who was still asleep, but she did not answer. When Gloria went to touch her, she felt stiff. Her skin had small, dark, blotchy patches all over, and her hands were curled up close to her chest. The villagers were all quiet inside as the blinding light came through the door's opening. It took a while to adjust their eyes since they had been sitting in darkness for so long.

One by one, they started to exit the truck. Anita, along with two others, were unable to make the long, hard journey. The mother with the baby was slow to exit. She was holding on to her baby so tightly while exiting with a blank stare in her eyes. Joaquin thought to himself, *What a good baby.* The baby hadn't cried in the past couple of days, and Joaquin just assumed it was a good baby. Everyone else around her knew what happened. As they passed her, they would put a hand on her shoulder and tell her, *"Lo siento."*

That woman had lost everything. She had lost her husband a few years ago, and with nowhere to go, she had stayed in the village with her family. It wasn't until one evening when she was coming home from another village, where she had been visiting relatives, that she was stopped by a small patrol of PCH members. They first walked past her; then one turned and asked if she needed help going home. When she said no, they became more outright with what they wanted. They asked if she was married and could they take her out sometime. She quickened her pace, trying to avoid their advances. They continued to pursue her until she was almost to the clearing where more people were. That's when they stopped her and began groping her and forcing themselves on her. One of them grabbed her by the hair and pulled her into a thicker part of the wooded area. Two others followed as one stood watch. The other two ripped her blouse and tore her dress, trying to get to her. This assault went on for an hour—or, to her, a lifetime—as they each took her. Laughing and spitting in her face as they entered her over and over again. When they finished, they left her there helpless and unable to move for fear of what they might try and do. She lay there hoping they wouldn't come back, but unable to move due to what just happened.

A month following the assault she noticed she did not get her menses. She was afraid to tell others that she may be pregnant because when they heard of the assault many people, including her mother and some family, blamed her for it. She did not have a good relationship with her mother, so telling her was out of the question. She hid it from everyone and moved on her own to the village she was in before leaving on the truck. She had just had the baby when she heard about the truck leaving for America. With everything that she had endured, and even after losing her baby, when she got out of the truck, she just started walking away. The truck had parked in the mountainous areas of where they were because it gave them some cover. As that woman held her baby, not saying anything to anyone, she simply walked off the side of the mountain where the road was. Joaquin and his mother had just got down from the truck when that woman took her baby and walked off the side of the road. Everyone was in shock and crying from the sight of what they witnessed. No one would have thought this trip would be so difficult and require so much of each of them.

"Wait! *¡QUÉ ACABAS DE DECIR!* What did you just say?" Gloria asked. "Where are we if we're not in America!!"

Chapter 3

The Vultures

"Hey! *¿Estás bien?*" Joaquin heard in the distance. A hard bump caused him to hit his head on the window, which snapped him out of his daze right away. He hadn't realized that he wasn't paying any attention to what was going on around him.

The man sitting next to him asked again, "*¿Estás bien?* Are you okay?"

Joaquin simply nodded his head yes and adjusted his sitting. The bump had caused him to slip, and he was slouching down a bit too much. Plus, the chain around his waist was digging into his back sitting that way. Once he sat back upright, he felt immediate relief in his back from that chain burying itself into his skin.

The caravan of buses left El Paso, en route to another holding facility somewhere near Eagle Pass, to pick up more people. The ride wouldn't have been so bad if there were some nice scenery to look at, but in this part of Texas all you get is dry, flat land with an occasional nopal. So, getting lost in your thoughts was pretty easy for the majority of the passengers. Looking around, Joaquin can see the all-too-familiar look of defeat on the faces of the others. Most gave up everything to try and come to America in order to help their families. Some came with their families, only to lose them to the heat, starvation, or killing by bandits. The looks on their faces ask the question, "Was it worth it? Did I do the right thing? I wonder if my family will be okay?"

That driver who smuggled those villagers out of Honduras was not as good a person as they assumed. Even though he stopped working for the PCH, he had started working for himself as an independent transporter. What he would do is find local villagers trying to escape from Honduras and tell them he could get them out. Once he had them, he would take them to a place in Mexico where they would be forced to work off their debt in a factory or warehouse. Those that refused, well that was a simple fix. There was an endless supply of people wanting to escape from Honduras, and he knew how to get them there. The companies he supplied didn't care where the people came from, so long as they had workers to keep production moving. They were kept in a gated pueblo near the companies. All who came to work had a debt that needed to be paid. The majority of the people had no money, so they could only work off what they owed. It would take years before Gloria could pay off her debt.

Once off the truck and crying over the woman who had walked off the side of the mountain, the Hondurans could see a bus with armed men waiting. The villagers were told to head towards the bus, and they would be told what to do. Some of the villagers pleaded and cried to not do this to them and to let them go. The driver had no remorse at all and pushed them in that direction.

The armed men started yelling for everyone to be quiet and to get in line. In line, they started binding their hands together and then to one another in groups of four. This was so they could still sit on the bus, two to a seat. They tied their wrists very tight, almost cutting circulation off to their hands. When some would start trying to resist, they would be struck in the head with a club or the back of a gun. This would motivate the others to not resist. It only took a few who resisted, their foreheads coated with their blood and seeping into their eyes; no one continued to plead or speak.

Gloria and Joaquin were tied to another woman and her young son about the same age as he. They were escorted into the bus and sat down with his mother in the middle, tied to the other mother. Joaquin, scared but not showing much emotion, just sat and gazed out the dirt-covered windows. He looked on as the driver of the truck they had been on and two other men dragged bodies out of the back and tossed them to the ground.

Gloria held Joaquin close and just kept saying, "We will get to America, *mijo*; don't you worry. We will get there."

All Joaquin said to his mother was "I'm sorry, Momma. If I had my sword, I could've protected you."

She just kissed him on the forehead and squeezed him tighter.

The last things Joaquin saw before they left that place were the older woman Anita being thrown over the side of the mountain and the men giving high fives to each other.

Five years passed, and Gloria was working hard in a factory that provided cocoa leaves to some soda-making company. They would ship the leaves in from Peru, and from there they would break it down for a company in the United States. Based on how long she worked and how much time she put in each day, Gloria figured how long she would have to work to pay off her debt so that they could leave. She knew they would be there a while, so she had Joaquin enrolled at the nearby school. They had these schools in place to make the people feel as though they are not captive, but actually working and helping. He started very late, but Joaquin was a quick learner, and it didn't take long for him to catch up with his peers. There were fewer than twenty kids in the whole pueblo, all roughly around the same age.

The woman and child they had arrived with became really close to Gloria. The boys also became good friends and could always be found together, getting into trouble or running around. Silvia was the woman's name, and she actually grew up a few towns over from where Gloria and Joaquin stayed before leaving Honduras. She was ten years younger than Gloria, but their sons were the same age, so it gave them something in common. Silvia and Gloria made sure that, once they were settled in the pueblo, they were close to one another so they could help each other out, especially with the boys.

Her husband had drowned while saving her son, Felipe, one rainy season. The river was high and moving very quickly. Felipe and some of his cousins were playing nearby on some rocks while his father was fishing for that evening's meal. The rocks were pretty slippery, and Felipe stepped on one, lost his footing, and fell into the moving river. The other children called out for help, and his father quickly jumped into the river without hesitation. He was able to grab Felipe as he was passing by and hold on to him. He tried to swim to shore, but the current under the surface was much faster than what he could see on top. He just held on, hoping to find a spot where they could grab hold of something to pull themselves onto the riverbank.

Almost a mile or so down the river, there were some larger rocks, and the father figured they could latch on to one and hold on till they were rescued. As they passed one, he told Felipe to grab on to a rock, hold on for dear life, and not let go until someone saved him. Felipe reached out and was able to grab the rock and didn't let go. His father attempted to grab one, but he slipped right off. In doing so, it turned him around, and he couldn't see where he was going. He smacked his head on a different rock. Felipe only saw his father as he washed away with his facedown in the water. He never saw him again. After that, Felipe would never go swimming in any water unless it was waist-high and still.

Silvia told Gloria one evening that she was approached by *El Guardián*, who was seeing if she needed anything; he told her that if she ever needed help, she could come directly to him. Gloria tried telling her that it wasn't worth her asking for his help, especially with the rumors that were spread throughout the pueblo. The last thing Gloria wanted was for something to happen to Silvia or Felipe, especially if Silvia got pregnant.

They had regulations against women having children since a pregnant woman could not work after a certain time, and someone not working slowed production. Those who came with children were placed in a section of the pueblo where the younger ones could be taught basic schoolwork until they became of age to work. In the unfortunate case where a woman was pregnant, she was forced to terminate it or worse.

They were told a story of a woman who refused to kill her baby. They brought her out in the middle of the pueblo. She was stripped naked and tied to a post. They carved a letter *P* on her forehead for *puta* and left her there. Those who tried to give her food or water were shot. It took about three days before the vultures began circling around, waiting for their next meal. After about the sixth or seventh day, she was almost lifeless as starvation and dehydration had completely taken over. Even moving her eyelids burned more energy than she had.

The vulture that had been sitting on the post above her came down and poked at her skin a few times, trying to assess if its meal was ready. Those pokes caused her skin to tear open, exposing the flesh that they wanted. The woman was motionless to the pokes. She was past the point of feeling anything that the vulture was doing. Other vultures that had been patiently waiting dropped down to join their companion. They said it took three days for them to finish eating that woman. The men who tied her up had a wager as to how long it would take. Since then, none of the women refused to do what they were told, or they would become the next wager.

The men of the pueblo, who were gone most of the day, worked in the forest, growing crops for food and other types of crops that were demanded of them. The women mainly worked in the factory, as they were quicker with their hands and neater with what they did. The work wasn't as physically demanding as in the fields, so the men mostly came home late in the evening. The few children just stayed in the pueblo area or went to school.

Gloria had finished her shift and asked to speak to whom they called "*La Guardián*." The warden was the man who made sure that all those in the pueblo were doing their jobs and kept track of all their debts. He had other men who worked for him who would patrol and make sure no one was planning on escaping or causing any trouble. Gloria came to the warden and pleaded her case, showing how much she had worked and telling him that she should have more than enough to be freed, plus a little more for the extra work she did.

The warden sat quietly for a moment and reached for his cigar that he had burning on his desk. He took a deep drag and slowly let it out before speaking. "*Sí*, Senora Gloria, you have worked many years with us and have worked enough hours for your freedom." He paused to puff on his cigar again. "But what about young Joaquin? He hasn't worked, and you definitely don't have enough time or money for him."

Despair took over Gloria because there was no way she would leave her son behind, and the thought that she would have to work many more years made her knees give way, and she was sick to her stomach. She immediately pleaded with the warden and asked if there was anything else she could do to secure their release.

He told her yes, that she needed to work more and harder, and that the time would come when they could leave.

She turned and left, feeling as though she had signed her death sentence. Thoughts of never making it to America flooded her mind.

Before she left, the warden called out to her, "So, I've noticed you don't have a husband and aren't with anyone. I could maybe cut some of your debt off if you are willing to do something for me."

With Gloria in her early forties, she hoped he wasn't implying what she was thinking he was. She had heard rumors that he was a filthy man and would take women and offer them nice things or clear some of their debt if they would do sexual things with him. He would never force himself on them, but if they wanted what they asked for, they would have to freely give themselves to him. "What would you have me do?" Gloria asked.

"Oh, nothing you haven't done before," he said with a smile before taking another puff of his cigar. He got up from his chair, came very close to her, and placed the side of his face to hers. *"Yo quiero probarrr,"* he said, making sure to roll that last R longer, before taking her earlobe into his mouth and sucking on it.

She could practically taste the stench of an old cigar and cheap whiskey smell that filled her nose as the sweat from his cheeks dripped onto her face. The chills that were sent through Gloria enraged her. She was unsure what to do at that moment, but her body took over; she kneed him in the groin and scratched him across the face.

The warden, very angry, grabbed Gloria by the hair and punched her in the face multiple times until she lost consciousness. He threw her to the ground and kicked her in the abdomen a couple of times and then ordered that she be tied to the pole as a reminder to anyone who tried to bite the hand that fed them.

The men took Gloria out of the office and dragged her to another room where they each took turns with her. They waited until she woke up for them to start, and they would beat her again until she passed out. This was done three times before they left her naked and took her by the hair and dragged her to the pole to tie her there.

Crowds grew as they brought Gloria to the cement pillar in the center of the pueblo. It hadn't been used in many years, but the eerie feeling about that pillar was always there. No one would go near it; they would always look away from it and do the *signo de la cruz* out of respect for the woman who died attached to it.

Joaquin was in class when all the commotion started. People were running towards the gathered crowds, and even the children all left the school to see what was happening. There was a good-sized crowd, and Joaquin couldn't see very well. So, he pushed his way through, trying to get a better view.

The warden came out enraged, bloody scratches across his face. He yelled to the crowds, "This is what I get for looking after you? This is how you repay me?"

Still unable to see, Joaquin moved closer to the front. With his heart racing in anticipation, time and movement stopped immediately as he moved past the last person in his way. Her face was unrecognizable from all the beatings, but Joaquin saw the shoes she was wearing and knew it was his mother.

He screamed out, hoping that it would stop the warden, but as he tried to run to his mother, the warden pulled out his gun. It was as if everything were moving in slow motion. You could almost hear the clicking of the gun from where Joaquin was as two shots fired off. Just before the bullets hit, he saw his mother look towards him and reach as if she could hold him one last time. The left side of her head was scattered all over the cement pillar, and her body slumped over on her side.

Like a log hitting him, Joaquin felt the air being sucked out of his chest. His whole life was his mother. She had been with him through everything that they encountered. She was his protector. The one who showed him how to do almost everything growing up. To whom would he turn now? He would never again see the smile on her face every morning and feel her hug and kiss on his forehead. She would always call him *mi vida* before she set off to work. All of that was taken away in an instant.

The bright, hot sun was blinding as he tried to open his eyes. A man standing over Joaquin with a large stick in his hand had a sly grin on his face. Joaquin then realized that the pain and air leaving his chest was from a man who hit him with that large stick when he attempted to run to his mother. Joaquin coughed and held his arms to his chest in pain, but nothing compared to the pain of his mother being taken from him in front of his eyes.

Joaquin buried his pain with the anger that rose up inside of him. The sight of his lifeless mother was more than he could bear. Her face was unrecognizable with all the bruising and swelling from the constant punching, along with the two holes from the warden and his pistol. The crowd around him and there at the pueblo was silent. Everyone was shocked at the horror that they'd just witnessed. Many of the villagers looked away from the sight because nothing like this had happened in such a long time.

At fifteen, Joaquin was smaller than most kids his age, and, being so small, he appeared much younger, which kept him from being pulled into the fields and jungle with the men. Many of the other boys were being sent out there once they were strong enough to carry a bushel. The lack of strength and height didn't not stop Joaquin when the rage needed to escape. He wanted revenge, and no one and nothing was going to stop him. He looked around for a split second to see if there was anything he could find to help him with the assault. The only thing was the stick that was used on him. The man had tossed it to the side after hitting Joaquin with it, and it was close enough for him to pick up and strike with. The tears he had in his eyes blurred his vision slightly, but Joaquin knew whom he was going after and did not need to see that well to do it.

With the stick in his hand and his target in sight, he ran as fast and as hard as he could toward the warden. No one else seemed to be there, and the tunnel in that direction was clear. As he got closer to the warden, he saw the happiness his mother once had and the smile she would always have on her face. Moments they shared together rushed through Joaquin's mind because he knew those would be the last ones they would have as a family.

The warden hadn't even paid much attention to Joaquin as he was running towards him with a stick. When the warden did turn, it was too late. Joaquin swung as hard as he could and with all the strength he could muster in his body. The stick found a nice, soft spot on the side of the warden's face and split the skin open all the way to the bone, crushing the eye socket as well. This caused the warden to grab his face and fall to his knees. Joaquin had another chance to strike him since the warden's head was down, and he was on his knees. As Joaquin wound up for the, hopefully, fatal blow to the man who had taken his mother from him, he thought to himself, *This is for my mother and all those you have wronged and taken advantage of.* Before that final blow came, Joaquin's mind went black.

The sound of an owl startled Joaquin out of the blackness he experienced. When the cloudiness in his head cleared a little, he noticed he was chained up to the same pillar his mother was. One of his eyes was crusted shut from the blood that had dried after coming from the big gash on the top of his forehead. Questions as to what happened and how he got there rushed in quickly. His last memory was standing over the warden, ready to hit him in the back of the head for doing what he did to his mother.

Unfortunately, he was not able to deliver that much-wanted hit. One of the men who worked for the warden had stopped the assault by shooting in the direction of Joaquin, aiming for his head. The bullet grazed his head, but stopped Joaquin and knocked him unconscious. The men didn't continue shooting at the small child, for fear that it would cause the villagers to stop working after all they'd already witnessed. So they tied him to the pillar and decided to let the vultures decide his fate.

A headache like no other he'd ever felt before woke Joaquin fully when he tried to move and see where he was. This pain made him wince, and he grabbed his head, not knowing of the open wound he had on his forehead. This sent a pain shooting all the way into his stomach, making him vomit yellow bile. It was dark all around, so he knew it was nighttime. He was just unsure what time it was. It was quiet, and no lights were on, so he assumed everyone was sleeping. With the pain from his head and because it was so dark, Joaquin decided to just wait till morning to see what he could do. Especially since he was tied up and unable to move very much or think clearly.

The morning traffic from the villagers and their gasps as they passed by woke Joaquin. He was trying to remember what happened when he looked over to his left and saw his mother there. Pale-white skin, eyes swollen shut, and blood covering all of what was left of her face. He looked at where the pillar was covered with her blood and bone fragments from her head. Some flies had already feasted on the open flesh of his mother's face, which was too much for him. He tried to swat them off, but accidentally hit her and noticed the hollow thud. Her skin was no longer soft and warm, but stiff and cold. Seeing his mother this way, so close, and his inability to do anything made him pass out from anxiety.

Two days later, as if from a far-off distance, he felt someone tapping him, asking if he was okay. When he did not respond, they tapped a little harder and asked again. When he opened the eye that wasn't crusted shut, he was met with feathers in his face and squawking from a vulture that had started picking at the dried wound on his forehead. He tried moving to push the heavy bird off him, but he didn't have much strength or energy due to not having food or water for the past few days. It was enough, however, to startle the bird, and it moved off his face and turned to where the other birds were.

It took him a moment to realize that the birds were on top of his mother. He mustered the remaining strength he could to kick at the birds since his hands were tied up. The kick scattered the vultures; they lingered close, but stopped tearing the flesh from his mother. Joaquin looked on in utter shock as most of the flesh from his mother's face was gone and the inside of her stomach was hanging out. Portions of her feet were missing, and she just no longer resembled the woman who would make him his special breakfast every weekend.

Why is this happening? What should I do? Is this it for me? These were all questions that kept rolling in his head. He tried looking around and only saw villagers closing their eyes to the sight of his once mother and Joaquin tied to the pillar. There were a few who sat far off, crying and looking on at this image of what happened to those who challenged the warden. He saw the men walking around with their guns, almost as if daring someone to come to Joaquin and his mother's aid.

Joaquin almost accepted his fate as he saw the vultures making their way back to the meal before them. Due to his lack of energy and will, he started fading out and losing consciousness. It was then he heard something in the distance. He opened his eye again, hoping to see what he was hearing. There was nothing there, and in disappointment he began fading again.

The sound became louder and more frequent. At first Joaquin thought it was his imagination, but then he saw the armed men look in the same direction from which he heard the sound. Commotion started within the village, and Joaquin noticed the armed men on their walkie-talkies and running towards the sounds. He almost spent all of his energy trying to stay awake, but he was fading.

The vultures flew away quickly, all at once. The sounds he was hearing started getting closer and closer. They finally jolted him awake as they seemed right next to him. He was then able to make out what he was hearing. Someone was shooting at the armed men, and explosions were filling up the pueblo. In complete exhaustion, Joaquin looked on at what was happening before him. It was difficult to make out because his vision was so blurry. Many armed men in dark-blue uniforms and a white stripe across their chests had these big, long guns; they flooded the pueblo and killed all the men who were holding the villagers. The people were happy and cheered, for they knew they had been saved.

Even with all the cheering and explosions going on, Joaquin was dropping in and out of consciousness. He couldn't make out what was happening or when he was taken from the pillar.

Chapter 4

Sister Ana

The bus pulled up to a closed gate, and the other buses that followed behind stopped inches from each other. An officer who was sitting in a small shack with the air conditioning blaring on high picked up his hat and adjusted his pants as he stood up. The weight of his duty belt caused his pants to fall a bit. When the officer walked out of the shack, his breathing immediately became labored, and sweat started beading up on his forehead from the heat. With a clipboard tucked under his arm, he walked over to the bus and asked the driver for the paperwork. He walked back into the shack and made a few phone calls, verifying, before allowing the buses to proceed. Once the documents were verified, the gate officer pushed the button to open the main gate and waved the bus through. Only one bus could go through the main gate at a time, so the process had to be repeated two more times.

The sound of the main gate's opening and closing had Joaquin coming back from where his thoughts had taken him. This stop was only to pick up more people who had been caught coming over the border earlier in the week. No need for those already on the bus to get down at this time. After the main gate, there was another gated area where the detainees were waiting outside for their ride to the next facility. As they pulled up, Joaquin could tell that these people weren't your ordinary villagers. These were all men who had tattoos all over their bodies and faces. Most with shaved heads and wearing red uniforms.

The color of uniforms indicated what level of security you required. The majority of people who were caught had to put on blue uniforms. That color was for people who didn't have any prior records; the only law they had broken was crossing the border. Others had to wear orange, which meant they had a minor record or had been caught a few times already. Some misdemeanors, but nothing serious. Then, you have the ones who were wearing red. Those individuals had committed serious crimes, either in the United States or in another country. They had to be separated from the other individuals because they may pose a threat. There was a portion of the bus in the front that was gated and separate from the remainder of the seats. That area was for those who were in red. As they were escorted onto the bus, a couple of the men would make whistling noises and blow kisses towards the other people in the bus.

Joaquin remembered not too long ago having to wear a red uniform, but thankfully he now only had to wear orange. Once they were seated, the officers conducted a count and name check from the bracelets they had to wear. After the guards were certain the detainees were all there, the bus began to leave again. Joaquin hadn't really looked at any of those men as they were entering the bus. His mind was still someplace else. His mother was everything to him, and when she was taken from him, he was unsure how he was going to be without her.

Joaquin woke up in what he thought was a hospital. Going into his arm, he had a tube that was attached to a bag of liquid above his head. He also had a thin tube connected to his nose and felt something lightly blowing through it. It itched as he was becoming more aware and fear, along with anxiety, started taking over. *Where am I, and how did I get here?*

He quickly glanced around and noticed the old stone-brick walls. Next to his bed, a small table with paint that was peeling off and faded. On top of it, there was a glass of water and a Bible, along with a vase and a small bunch of wild flowers that was clearly not enough to fill the vase. He looked up and saw a crucifix on the wall above his head. Light coming from a small window to his right lit up the room. The dust-filled rays shone on the heavy wooden door that was open.

Joaquin noticed someone walking by, and they had on the same clothes he would see when he went to Mass every Sunday. He tried moving, but was stopped by sore muscles and pain coming from his head. He stilled and just waited for the pain to go away before attempting to move again. As he lay there trying to remember what happened, there was a brief memory flash of something seen after an explosion. He recalled laying eyes on a being that, to him, resembled an angel, similar to those in the pictures he'd seen at the little church he and his mother would attend in Honduras. He could really only remember seeing this angel-like figure approaching him and then holding him as the pueblo was being overtaken by the men in uniform. Screaming and cries of joy from the villagers were everywhere as they beckoned the men in uniform to save them from the armed men. As Joaquin struggled to remember everything that occurred, he recalled, just before it all faded, more angelic beings had come and carried him away.

"*¿Cómo estás, mijo?*" a soft voice called out, startling Joaquin.

He turned to look towards where the voice was coming from. A person passed through the sunray shining from the window at just that right moment, but Joaquin was unable to see a face until they approached. The voice was calming, and it was not a voice he felt afraid of. When they stepped closer, the light faded behind them, and Joaquin was able to see who was speaking to him. It was a nun in white with blue borders, like the nuns from the church back in Honduras.

"*Hola, mijo, me llamo* Maria Ana, but you can just call me Sister Ana," she began as she started checking the bag above his head, fluffing his pillow, and checking the IV lines in his arms. She was very gentle and nice, Joaquin noticed, and always kept a smile on her face. *Very different from the nuns back in Honduras,* he thought. They were much older and never smiled. They would always spank Joaquin and his friends for just being boys and doing mischievous things.

Joaquin didn't answer her at first; he was still unsure where he was and how he got there. Plus, the fear of what he went through still hadn't left his mind. He felt safe, but didn't want to fully let his guard down, not knowing who was caring for him.

Sister Ana simply kept on with what she was doing. Then, another voice came from the door. This one was more stern and not as pleasing. In walked another nun, much older, and she had the all-too-familiar long face with no smile on it. "Well, how is he? I didn't send you in here to take your time," she barked, which caused Sister Ana to put her head down.

"*Perdóname*, Sister Maria Guadalupe, I am almost finished."

Joaquin immediately didn't like the older nun and started to become restless in his state.

"*Mira*, you're taking too long, and it's bothering him," Sister Maria Guadalupe stated as she rushed Sister Ana, who scurried out of the room without another word.

After a few days, Joaquin had built up enough strength and energy that he was sitting up on his own and speaking with Sister Ana. She had learned that he was fifteen years old and soon having a birthday. She told him that he was surprisingly small for his age, but that he seemed very bright, given that he only looked twelve. He explained to her where he was from and what he remembered happening before they found him. Sister Ana was roughly about Joaquin's mother's age, so he found it easier to speak with her. There were other nice nuns who would come in from time to time, but Sister Ana was the first one who was nice to him, so he opened up to her more. When he started telling her about his mother, tears filled his eyes, and Joaquin became quiet and was just thinking about how much he missed his mother.

Sister Ana told Joaquin that he was in a missionary hospital. "This used to be a church many years ago, but during the wartime they didn't have enough hospitals for the wounded, so they converted many churches into hospitals. After the war, many of them converted back into churches, but this one stayed as a hospital, and now we provide help when the army needs it or if they find someone like you who requires help." She went on to tell him that the Mexican Army had been finding pueblos, like the one where they found him, and freeing the people. They knew that these men were kidnapping people and forcing them to work in their factories, making them believe they were working off a debt. Unfortunately, they would never let them finish paying their debt.

What she didn't tell Joaquin was that, once they had finished paying their debt (which meant they could no longer work or were just too old), they would take them as a group and drive them away. The people assumed that they were being set free and allowed to continue on their journey, but that was not the case. The armed men would take them to a place in the jungle and line them up with burlap bags over their heads. They'd make them get on their knees and, one by one, shoot them in the back of the head. Their bodies would fall into this giant pit that was already piled up with other bodies. Once this happened, they would send for another fresh load of workers to begin the whole process over again.

Sister Ana then told him that the men they had been working for had been processing and making drugs from what they were doing there at that pueblo. They assumed they were just harvesting the cocoa leaves and prepping them for the soda company in America, but that was just the first process. It was sent off to another factory and processed to make a drug called cocaine. They used this lie of harvesting the leaves, even though this soda company stopped using it more than twenty years ago. They would tell people this to get them to work for them and promise that with all their hard work it would get them a trip to America since they were working for an American company. This gave the travelers hope, and they worked as hard as they could, only to be buried in the pit next to many others.

Joaquin was stunned with what he had just learned. This made him more upset about the whole situation. It really didn't matter what he or his mother did. They probably would've never left the pueblo and gone to America as his mother wanted. He sat there the remainder of the evening, quiet and unable to sleep.

The next morning, Sister Ana entered his room and seemed a little disconnected and worried. She paced back and forth, adjusting her head garment and not really smiling. This worried Joaquin because she hadn't told him what was going on. Finally, she stopped moving and spoke, "Joaquin, *mijo*. Sister Maria Guadalupe is coming to speak to you and you must not tell her your real age. If she knows that you are almost sixteen, she will have you taken from here. You are almost better now, and you will be able to go as you please. We need the beds for sick people, and she will want to fill up your bed as soon as possible. As long as she believes you are twelve, she will allow you to stay until you're sixteen. She is not an evil person, but she is very strict and likes to keep order in this facility. She doesn't allow people to stay past their time, in case they try to take advantage of us."

Joaquin had not thought of what he would do once he was better. He had been so lost in his grief, and in the company of the nuns, he hadn't even worried about what was to come next. Sister Ana left the room quickly, and it allowed Joaquin to think of what he was going to say to the other sister. If he stayed, what would he do, and how long could he pretend to be the age Sister Ana told him to be? On the other hand, if he revealed his actual age, he would have to leave. And then what? Where would he go, and what could he do with nothing? He waited in anticipation for Sister Maria Guadalupe to show, but she didn't that evening.

The next morning, Joaquin was excited to see Sister Ana come in, as she always had for the past three weeks, to check on him. The wound on his head was all healed, besides the scar and the tiny holes caused by the several stitches he'd needed. He had regained his full strength from the many days without food and water while being tied to the pillar. He still had some bruising on his chest and other parts of his body, but he was good to go if need be. He still hadn't decided what he was going to tell Sister Maria Guadalupe.

He could hear footsteps approaching and was ready with a smile on his face. The smile quickly faded as Sister Ana did not enter the room. Rather, it was Sister Maria Guadalupe. She had the usual straight, inexpressive look about her; she entered and stood at the end of the bed. "Sister Ana has been reassigned to another sickbed. Since you no longer require any medical attention, we need to figure out what to do with you," she began with a strong, yet calm, tone about her. "We have need of this bed, and you are well enough to be on your own without supervision." Joaquin sat quietly as she continued and only answered questions she asked. She questioned how he felt and how his head and eyesight were. Then she asked his age.

Joaquin had been thinking about his mother, what she wanted for them, and how she was determined to get to America. She would always tell him that there was nothing there for them and that they needed to start a new and better life in America. The land of the free and many opportunities.

"I asked you a question. HOW OLD are you?" she repeated as if speaking to someone who was hard of hearing.

He was upset that she had interrupted his thoughts of his mother. "I'm almost sixteen, and I need to get to America," he said with a sharp tone.

"Very well then, you will have your wish. You leave first thing in the morning. I will arrange the trip, and you will be on your way," Sister Maria Guadalupe stated and then turned and walked out of the room.

As soon as she left, the upset feeling Joaquin had when she interrupted his thoughts of his mother was quickly replaced with anxiety. *What was I thinking*? There was no way a young kid like him could make it there by himself. He wished he had someone there to speak with. Sister Ana was the only one he confided in, and she was no longer there.

That evening, Sister Ana had something she needed to report to Sister Maria Guadalupe. As she arrived at her office, the door was slightly open. She couldn't see anyone, but she could hear that Sister Maria Guadalupe was on the phone with someone. She put her ear closer to the door and tried to make out what she was saying.

"Yes, I have three for you. You can come pick them up in the morning. No, one is midthirties, and the other two are very young. Yes, they should be able to do what you need them to do. Only thing is, one of them is small for his age. Very well, I will have them ready for you."

Sister Ana was stunned by the conversation she just heard. She left immediately and ran towards Joaquin's room to tell him. In Joaquin's room, she was frantic and told him he needed to leave right now because of the phone conversation she just heard.

That startled Joaquin because he could see the look of terror and concern in her eyes. He quickly jumped out of bed and put on some clothes that Sister Ana had brought for him, along with a bag of a few things for him. She told him to wait for her, as she wanted to go alert the others, and she would show them a way out.

Joaquin started to get impatient. He had no idea what was happening with Sister Ana, and he was pacing back and forth in the room. He finally heard some footsteps, and they sounded as if they were moving very quickly, so he knew it had to be Sister Ana. Two armed men entered the room, followed by Sister Maria Guadalupe, with the same look on her face as always. Joaquin's heart sank, and a knot in his stomach nearly made him collapse at the sight of the armed men.

Sister Maria Guadalupe had taken over the facility nearly twenty years ago. She had initially started off by doing good for people. Many missionary excursions would go through her facility, and they would provide medical care for those who needed it. She employed many people of the church, and it became well known throughout the land that you could always go there and receive help. Over the years, the upkeep and supplies became scarce and expensive. She was finding it difficult to fund the projects she felt were God's work. She would light candles every night and pray for some miracle to help her.

One day some men came to her with suitcases full of money. They explained to her that she would receive more money than she knew what to do with so long as she provided them with men and boys over the age sixteen. At first, there was no way she could do such a thing, especially in the eyes of God. Repeatedly, she battled with herself over the proposal of those men. There was no way she could do such a thing to the people she vowed to serve and care for. Until one day she received a letter that they were closing down her facility due to lack of funds. She wouldn't let that happen and decided that she would use the men's money for good. Sister Maria Guadalupe convinced herself that, with all the good she would be able to do with the money, it would be okay to overlook the few men and boys who were taken. They would be used as mules and forced to cross over drugs to America. If they refused, they would meet the same fate as those in the jungles. So long as they did what they were asked, they would be rewarded with money and be released in America.

Joaquin didn't know what to do, so he did the first thing that came to mind. He tried to run away. He made it through the door and ran down a hallway in search of a way out. Besides using the bathroom and bathing in a nearby room, he had no idea where he was in the building or how to get around. There was another door down from the bathroom he remembered and headed that way. The armed men took after Joaquin, but not in any rush. They knew he was unable to get out. Joaquin came to that other door by the bathroom and tried to open it. It was locked. When he turned around, the armed men were already there waiting for him. As they came closer, Joaquin told himself he was not going down without a fight. He charged and tried to hit one of the men. They were much bigger and stronger than he and were able to subdue him easily.

He was still fighting and trying to escape when they brought out Sister Ana along with the other man and boy. They had Sister Ana tied with a rope around her neck and a gun to her head. The other two were bound at the wrists. Joaquin froze at the sight of Sister Ana. He didn't want anything to happen to her. "Please, don't hurt her! I won't fight anymore if you just let her go!" he pleaded with them. He stopped struggling and put his hands out in front of him so that he could be tied up.

The armed man holding Sister Ana let go of the rope from around her neck. Joaquin took that as a sign that his pleading and willingness to go freely was enough of a bargain for her freedom. The man who held Joaquin gave a nod to the one holding Sister Ana, and he untied the rope. She coughed loudly and rubbed her neck where the rope was squeezing tightly. She turned to Joaquin and gave an apologetic look.

Once tied, all three captives were escorted out. They left Sister Ana with an armed man until they cleared the building. As the three of them walked down the hall, they turned a corner. That is when Joaquin heard the single gunshot. It echoed through those stone hallways and sounded as if it would not end. The sound caused Joaquin to freeze, and tears immediately filled his eyes because he knew what happened. The armed men escorting them pushed him forward and giggled as they heard the sound of the gun going off.

As they exited the building, it began to thunder and lightning. Once they were placed into the truck, the rain started coming down really heavily. The last armed man who was in the building came out and got in the front with the others. Joaquin's heart was heavy with sadness. He couldn't believe that they would do that to Sister Ana. She had become his friend, and she died trying to protect him. He was hoping that this didn't become a frequent occurrence when someone got close to him. Already, at a young age, he had lost so many people in his life.

It was already dark by the time they left the missionaries' facility. Add to that the heavy rain, and the visibility on the road was very difficult for the driver. They had to cross through some very tough terrain, which included driving along the side of a mountain to get to where they were going. The driver had made this drive many times, so he had no worries as to where he was going.

The rain picked up and the winds became stronger. The road was even more dangerous. Joaquin and the other two sitting in the back had little cover from the rain, and with the truck sliding back and forth, they were having a difficult time holding on. The driver, not trusting the road along the mountain, decided to take a different road that led farther down but was not as dangerous. He rarely ever took this route, as it took longer, but with the current weather conditions he decided it would be the safest for them. What he didn't account for was the rising waters and how quickly the roads filled up with water. The men inside told him to turn around and go the usual way. He didn't listen and kept pushing forward.

As they were driving, he couldn't see the giant low-water area covering the road, and they drove right into it. The truck immediately went dead as the water was too high for it. The water continued to rise, and they quickly realized they were in the path of a stream. It took the truck along with other debris and trees in its path. Another vehicle had already been swept in the current, but no one was in it. There was nothing they could do, being trapped in the truck, and nowhere they could go. They lost control of the truck and were at the mercy of the current. Due to the darkness and not being able to see anything, they were not prepared for what was coming at them.

Since it rarely rained in this region, the amount of rain that poured down so quickly caused a mudslide. It had giant boulders it picked up along its destructive path, and the current caused the truck to run right into this mudslide. Several boulders hit the truck, almost immediately causing the truck to topple over. The men inside the truck were pinned and had no way of getting out. Joaquin and the other two were being tossed around with nothing to hold on to. They had no idea if they should stay inside or take their chances outside and hopefully live through the mudslide. Another boulder hit the truck, breaking the windows and quickly filling the inside, where the armed men were, with mud and water. There was no escaping, even as hard as they tried. The truck was still being tossed around when the three captives somehow were thrown from the truck, out the back.

Joaquin tried moving in the mud, but it was so heavy it wouldn't allow him to move, as if he were in water. He tried reaching for the other two captives, but they were swallowed up in the mud. Joaquin felt himself getting sucked under, but looked around for anything he could grab hold of. He reached out several times, trying to grab branches to pull himself out, but was not successful. The branches either broke from his weight or the mudslide took them along with them. Finally, there was a tree he was able to reach and hug. He was barely able to hold on because he was exhausted. With his last ounce of strength, he was able to pull himself up out of the dragging mud and farther up in the tree.

The rains continued for what seemed like hours, causing the mud to thin and eventually just flow through, leaving only the large, heavy stream of water. Eventually, that slowed as well. Joaquin managed to settle himself on the tree so that he could sit, rest, and allow the water level to fall so that he could climb down from the tree. Even through all this, he joked to himself, *"Podría vivir como un mono."* Maybe he could live like a monkey. He chuckled and rested his eyes for a bit. Either way, he knew he needed to figure out where he was and to find his way north.

Joaquin was woken by someone tossing rocks at him. "HEY! What are you doing in our tree?"

Chapter 5

Mi Vida

The younger man sitting next to Joaquin started talking to him. He initially wasn't paying attention because he was thinking about some of the things he had gone through, but Joaquin eventually figured he didn't want to be rude. The younger man's name was Wilber Cruz, and he was born in Honduras, but his family moved to Mexico years back, before trying to cross into America. Wilber didn't spend much time in Honduras as a child. He went on about the wife and children he had back home in Mexico. How he was hoping that they wouldn't send him to Honduras because he didn't know anyone there, and he would have to find a way to Mexico. Just like most men who leave their families behind, he sent them money when he could and tried to save some in hopes of bringing them over so they could be together. This was the second time he was caught crossing over.

The first time he had been caught crossing in Rio Grande City. There is a low-water area that connects to a sewer, which leads right into America and comes out in one of the neighborhoods. The second time he was already here in America, but was picked up in a raid of a grocery store in El Paso. He had been living in the United States when that raid happened. Joaquin asked him if the trip through Mexico was rough for him and if he had encountered any problems.

Wilber said, "¡*Pues, tú sabes!* You know how it is. Traveling by bus and train has its ups and downs. It's hard on everyone who makes that trip. You never know what you're going to encounter on the road." He went on to tell Joaquin about how the group they traveled with almost ran out of water, but were saved by some ranchers who left water jugs in some places. Also, how one time they had to pay a few banditos to pass certain roads. Then, about the time when one of the men they were traveling with lost a leg; he was jumping on the train, but missed and got his leg caught. "You know, the same story as everyone who makes that journey," Wilber told him.

Joaquin simply nodded, and in his mind he thought, *Yeah, just like everyone's journey here.*

Another stone flew and this time hit Joaquin in the face. It startled him, and he almost fell from the tree. He had to catch himself; he reached and grabbed ahold of a branch near him.

"Hey! I said what are you doing in our tree? *Bajar de allí,*" a voice coming from below shouted.

Joaquin woke up fully, looked down, and saw a girl with another rock in her hand, ready to throw it at him. "Okay! Okay, wait. I'm coming down," he said and pleaded for her not to throw another rock at him. As he stood up, the tree and his feet were still covered in mud, so he lost his footing and fell out of the tree. The ground was soft from all the rain, and where he fell was still very muddy. The fall didn't hurt as much as the embarrassment.

The girl almost fell over from laughing so hard at the sight of Joaquin covered in mud and the sound he made when he fell. He attempted to stand up and make himself presentable, but she was laughing too much at him. She even let out a small snort while laughing. Joaquin quickly got annoyed at her laughing at him in such a vulnerable state. He tried stepping onto drier land, but his feet were stuck in the mud; the shoe he was wearing stayed in the mud and caused him to fall again. He heard another snort from her laughing, and the irritation was turning into more embarrassment. He no longer wanted to be the subject of ridicule, so he started to walk away.

"*Perdóname.* I'm sorry; don't go," she called out to him. "*Me llamo Cati,* and this is my family's farm you're on."

Joaquin stopped and turned to her. "I'm Joaquin, and I'm just trying to get to America. I didn't mean to trespass. I was caught in a mudslide, and your tree saved me," he explained quickly. "*Ay, Dios mío,* you were in that? We saw the mud and rushing waters coming, and thankfully it missed our home. We live just up the way over there. Come get cleaned up, and I'll find you some clothes you can change into," she offered to Joaquin.

He was getting ready to say "no, thank you" when a man, who turned out to be her father, rode up on a horse and told Joaquin to come to their house. Cati explained to her father what happened, so her father told Joaquin he could change and rest up at the house. What else could he say or do? Her father had a hunting rifle, and Joaquin had no strength or energy to argue or run. So he followed Cati back to the house.

As they were walking, he noticed that she had to be about his age. Her long skirt was dirty at the bottom from all the mud around, but she didn't seem the type who cared if she was dirty. Her blouse was neatly tucked in her skirt and bright white, with floral patterns all over. She had a single braid that held her thick hair, and it fell to the front of her on the right side. When she turned towards him, he could see that it reached all the way to her stomach. Her face was very soft and radiant.

Joaquin had never looked at a girl the way he was looking at Cati. Most of all, he couldn't stop staring at her eyes and smile. With all that he had gone through, it was as if those eyes and that smile made him forget it all. The loud snort of the horse made him snap back to paying attention to walking. When Joaquin looked up, he noticed her father looking at him with his stone-piercing eyes and straight face. Joaquin quickly looked away to avoid being killed by her father's stare.

Back at the house, in one of the barns, they showed Joaquin a bathroom the father used when he was too dirty from working the farm all day. He took a shower and was given some clean clothes that belonged to Cati's brother. As Joaquin entered the house, Cati and her mother were busy preparing lunch. She introduced Joaquin to her mother, and he was invited to sit so he could eat. There was a large table, but only four plates set out, so Joaquin just sat in the chair closest to him. Her father came in shortly after putting up the horse and took his boots off at the door. He walked up and gave Cati's mother a kiss on the forehead and tried to take his normal seat, but Joaquin was already sitting there. Joaquin looked around and saw those stone-cold eyes again and knew he should probably move. He decided to take the chair across from him to put some distance between them. He never knew a look could be that intimidating. If he hadn't been so tired and hungry, he probably would've just kept on his way instead of staying.

The mother and daughter both started asking Joaquin questions as to where he was from, how he got there, and why he was traveling alone. Joaquin never really talked about it before, especially with strangers he just met. So he simply told them that he was from Honduras and lost his mother at an early age. That he was an only child and had no other family, so he decided to go to America because that is what his mother wanted for him. He went on to say that he was on his way, passing through the area, when the rains started and he was caught in the mudslide; that's when Cati found him in the tree. His answers seemed to please them, so they didn't drill him with more questions. It was the typical reason why many left for America. Her father went from the piercing eyes and straight face, to crossing his arms over his chest. Joaquin wasn't sure if her father believed him or not.

Joaquin learned that Cati's older brother had gone off to work with her uncle at some factory a few years ago, but they hadn't heard from him in the past month or so. Cati's mother simply stated he was probably just working really hard and hadn't had time to call. This seemed to upset the father because he needed help on the farm, but her brother didn't want to be stuck on the farm his whole life. The father and son had a big falling-out, and he went off to work with his mother's brother. He was a man of few words and rarely showed any emotion after his son left. He blamed himself for pushing his son away. This left Cati's father to tend to the farm by himself. He occasionally had some helpers, but they came and went as they were just traveling through to get to America.

After lunch, Cati and her mother both told Joaquin that he could stay for the day and rest before he set off. Joaquin agreed and decided to lie down. The previous night's events had his body really sore, and he started to remember Sister Ana and how she died. Even though he was not present while she was killed, the image of her staring at him while the armed man pulled the trigger and her body slowly falling forward to the ground with her eyes still open in the direction of Joaquin caused him to snap out of his nap. It was nighttime already, and Cati jumped back as she was approaching to wake him up for dinner. He didn't realize he had been asleep for so long. He figured his body really needed it. For one thing, he was so glad Cati was the first thing he saw upon waking up.

The startle he gave her quickly turned into laughter. There it was again, the little snort sound she made when she laughed loudly. Joaquin thought to himself, *I could listen to that all day.*

Cati, trying to regain composure from the laughing, told Joaquin, "Dinner is almost ready, sleepyhead; come and eat." He felt a little embarrassed about scaring her that way and apologized repeatedly for it. She simply told him it was okay, that she got a good laugh out of it. As he watched her walk back up to the house, he saw her father in the window, staring with that same look again. This immediately made Joaquin turn and move from his view.

Back at the house, Joaquin walked in and everyone stopped speaking. Cati walked past with her melting smile that Joaquin couldn't get enough of; she was fixing the table for dinner.

"Sentarse; vamos a comer," Cati's mother tells him as she stirs something in a pan on the stove.

Joaquin obeyed and sat across from Cati's already staring father. Joaquin wondered if he ever blinked because, every time he looked at the man, he never saw a blink.

The quietness at the table was thickening with every passing moment. Cati's father finally spoke and asked Joaquin, "So, you left Honduras and made it all the way here with just that small bag you had draped on you when we found you?"

Before Joaquin could even think of an answer, the mother smacks the father on the shoulder and says, *"Déjalo en paz, viejo."* Leave him alone. That's all she said, and he went back to being quiet again.

During dinner, Cati came up with the idea that Joaquin should stay awhile to help on the farm, that her father could pay him, and, that way, Joaquin could save up for his trip to America. She argued that due to it being the rainy season, it was unsafe; he should wait for that to pass and then go. Her father started shaking his head no; he was against the idea. He claimed that Joaquin was too small and wouldn't be able to handle the work.

Joaquin just sat there, unsure what to say, because they both were making valid points. Joaquin didn't want to run into another mudslide, and he knew his physical limits. He was always smaller than most and looked younger, so he was never made to go work in the fields like the other boys his age. He also thought about being taken by another mudslide and was not ready for that to happen again.

Cati's father finished his meal and got up from the table, appearing to be upset at the discussion, and went to his room. The mother told Joaquin, "It's settled, *mijo*, you will stay until the wet season is over, and you may leave then if you wish. Now you must go and get some sleep; my husband wakes up really early and doesn't like to waste time."

Cati walked Joaquin out to where he would sleep in the barn and let him know not to worry about anything with her father. It didn't offer him much assurance, given the way her father had been staring at Joaquin, but her smile was enough for him to forget the piercing stare. She turned and left, and Joaquin just stood there watching Cati walk back to the house.

He went to lie down and noticed the bag he had when he left the missionary facility; his clothes had been washed and folded. He reached in the bag and pulled out a Bible and some other little book. There was a container with some food in it. A pencil and some blank paper. He was shaken when he reached in and pulled out the last remaining item in the bag—his father's pocketknife. Tears flooded his eyes and covered his cheeks as he sat there opening the knife. He thought he had lost it back at the pillar. Sister Ana had it and returned it to him in the bag she gave him just before losing her life.

That night, just like most nights since his mother's murder, Joaquin relived that moment. Now, he had the added images of Sister Ana's death making it difficult to sleep. He couldn't keep his eyes closed long without seeing the vultures laughing as they took turns eating his mother alive while she screamed for Joaquin to help her. He tried to reach out many times for her, but his hands were tied up. He saw over and over the warden shooting his mother and then shooting Sister Ana. Drowning in their own blood as they lay there looking at Joaquin, he could feel their blood sucking him in until eventually he woke up drenched in sweat just before he drowned as well.

Morning came quickly, and Joaquin was up before Cati's father since his dreams tended to wake him. Her father was surprised when he came out and Joaquin was there waiting for him. "Well I suppose we better get started if we are to finish sometime today. Go and grab the lopping shears and the small, sharp shovel with a long handle on it," he instructed Joaquin.

Joaquin could sense a bit of irritation in the man's voice, but didn't want to say that he had no idea what those things were. He simply nodded his head and went to look for the tools.

Cati was out there to see them off and met Joaquin in the shed where the tools were. He was looking at the tools for a moment when Cati asked, "You have no idea what he asked for, do you?" He chuckled and shook his head. She reached out and gave him what he needed before her father came searching for him.

He thanked her and gave her a hug. She smelled of lavender, and he didn't want to let her go. As he hugged her, she put her right hand on his left cheek very tenderly and gave him a slow, lingering kiss on his right cheek. This action sent a shock wave of emotions through him, and he had no way of responding. He was frozen in place and was afraid to move. His feet felt so heavy, and his forehead felt as if someone had poured water over his head. The smile she gave him as she moved away was a look he would always remember.

Cati's father was busy getting another horse ready for Joaquin. When he was finally able to move and remember what he was in the shed for, it was as if Joaquin were walking on clouds as he left the shed and headed towards Cati's father. Her father, with the same stoic face, was patiently waiting for Joaquin when he finally showed up with the tools he'd requested.

They set off for a tour of the farm and to learn what Joaquin would be doing during his time there. It wasn't a very big farm, but it did have quite a bit of crops growing on it. He learned that the family provided many crops for many pueblos, and Cati's father liked to rotate the crops and grow different ones based on the season, keeping things fresh and providing a good variety for customers. When he saw all the different types of things grown on the farm, Joaquin realized that Cati's family seemed to do pretty well for that region, but they stayed very humble.

Cati's father finally told Joaquin, "Well, now that you're planning on being here for a while, you can call me Señor Hernandez."

Joaquin agreed, and they continued on the tour of the farm. As they were ending the tour, Joaquin noticed a patch of land, which was separate from the rest of the farm, had agave plants growing for many rows. Joaquin asked, "*Y los agave*, what are they being grown for?"

Señor Hernandez had waited to show this part of the farm last because that was where he mainly wanted Joaquin to help. Joaquin was led to another smaller barn that had a blank banner above the door. "This is something I've been working on for a few years, and one day I hope to have it become something everyone in the world loves," Señor Hernandez stated. His whole attitude changed when he was talking about what he had brewing in that barn. He wasn't the same stoic man whom Joaquin had kept seeing from the moment he arrived. Joaquin could tell that this was something Cati's father was very passionate about.

He gave Joaquin a sip of the liquid, and he, almost immediately, spit it out. He hadn't tasted anything like it before. Señor Hernandez laughed at the sight of him spitting it out. Joaquin told him it stung a little going down.

"Yes, I know. I've been trying to come up with something that best represents, some symbol. I thought of a snake, a scorpion, or a wasp. They all sting, but I just need to think of the best one to represent my creation." He then told Joaquin, "I've been trying to make this tequila that is different from others, one that will be perfect for anyone to drink."

For the remainder of the day, Joaquin was taught how to harvest and peel the agave plants. The tools he was told to retrieve were part of a process and were needed to peel back the leaves. It took several tries to get the hang of it, but Cati's father was very impressed at how quickly Joaquin picked it up. The remainder of the jobs around the farm consisted of going around the farm and making sure that nothing was happening to the crops.

After the tour, Señor Hernandez gave Joaquin instructions on what he expected on a daily basis and told him he wasn't going to be babysitting him. If he didn't get the job done as he was supposed to, he would find himself with no place to stay. He showed Joaquin a small shack far away from the house and told him that it was where he would be staying.

Time passed, and Joaquin saved all that he could. Before he knew it, he hadn't even realized that five years had come and gone. He almost never thought about going to America. Cati and he had become very close, and Joaquin even asked her father if he could court her. Joaquin was a late bloomer and no longer looked like a little boy. He had grown close to six feet tall, which made him taller than most of the villagers. The newfound growth came in handy working on the farm and dealing with the agave plants. The nightmares were still lingering, but being with Cati helped him get through it much easier.

Her father at first was not happy about the situation because he lived too close, and to keep an eye on them all the time was difficult. He did, however, open up more to Joaquin, and they would often spend most of the day talking about the tequila and what he should call it. On the way home from a hot day, they noticed a vehicle at the house. Upon their arrival, the ladies were excited and couldn't wait to tell them the news. Word was sent to them that Cati's *tio* from her mother's side was having a *quinceañera* for his daughter and wanted everyone to be there. Her mother wasn't excited for the party, as much as the anticipation of seeing her son, since he still hadn't reached out to them. It had been over five years since they last heard from him, and she just wanted to know how he was doing. They sent many letters and made some phone calls, but heard nothing. The party would be within two weeks, so they started making arrangements to go. Señor Hernandez made sure that the farm was looked after for their time away. Joaquin was not even considering going until one evening, while at dinner, Cati's mother asked him if he had anything nice to wear. He didn't, so he had to go into town and find something suitable for the *quinceañera*.

It was a two-hour drive to her *tio*'s house, so they left as early as they could to avoid being late for the ceremony. By the time they arrived, there were so many people you would have thought he'd invited the whole country. Joaquin had seen a few *quinceañeras* before, but nothing like the spectacle before him. There was a petting zoo with many different animals, two live bands playing, and her *tio* even had cockfights going on. It was unlike anything Joaquin had ever seen before.

"Who is your uncle? How is he that rich?" he asked Cati.

She simply chuckled and said that her uncle could be a little extreme with his parties at times, but that he was really a great person. He always helped them when they needed it and never asked for any money back. "Hopefully we can meet him soon. He is always surrounded by people, and it can be difficult to even say hello to him."

Joaquin still was in awe of everything he witnessed at the party. They walked around for a while until they found where much of her family was. They were all very happy to see each other because it had been so long since they had gotten together. Telling each other about those who had passed and who were really sick quieted the mood a bit. Then, a large group of people were walking, and Joaquin, being taller than most now, was still having a difficult time seeing who was in the large crowd moving across the way. He then saw the big, overwide dress and a few armed men walking beside the girl wearing it; Joaquin realized that must be the daughter. He couldn't make out their faces because they were too far away. As they got closer, the crowds around them grew larger. There was no way they would be able to say hello now with that crowd.

There was something vaguely familiar about the man walking next to the girl in that giant dress. Joaquin tried to get a better view, but, every time he would move to see him, someone else would be in the way. Joaquin stopped trying to see. Once the ceremony ended and all the eating started, they were all called over to come say hello to Cati's *tio* and his daughter. Her *tio* had been sitting with his family and other men at this very large table that could seat at least twenty people, it looked like to Joaquin. Joaquin lingered in the back with Cati as a few family members said hello first. Joaquin was still trying to get a good look at the man, but he couldn't. As they moved closer, Joaquin could swear that a laugh sounded very familiar. He couldn't recall where he had heard it, but it made him feel uncomfortable for some reason. Joaquin kept his eyes down as Cati's parents said hello first.

"*Pues*, let me take a look at my beautiful niece!"

As her parents moved aside, Joaquin looked up. You would have thought a ghost ran through him and stayed there without moving. Joaquin was frozen with fear. He looked at her *tio*'s face and knew immediately who that was. The scars on his face and the eye that had turned white brought back that day almost immediately. The same smile the man had after shooting Joaquin's mother was burned into Joaquin's mind and could never be forgotten. Anticipation turned to fear and hate when Joaquin looked upon the man who had killed his mother. Joaquin wanted to jump over the table and finish what he started, and he wouldn't have cared what happened to him. But then he started thinking about what would happen to everyone else, and he couldn't bear to lose anyone else who was close to him.

"Joaquin, don't be rude; say hello."

Cati's voice snapped him back, but the rage he felt was still in his eyes. Joaquin thought, for sure, the man would remember him, but Joaquin had changed a lot since being tied to that pillar and watching his mother become a meal. His anxiety had taken over, and he was sweating more than after a hard day's work. He let out a soft, quick *hola*, turned, and walked away.

How can this be? Is he really here alive? Joaquin had been told that all the armed men were killed and no one survived. He couldn't concentrate and kept pacing around, unsure of what to do. His feelings were all over the place, and he had no idea how to react or what to do.

Cati could see that there was something wrong with Joaquin and walked after him. Her *tio* didn't even notice, let alone hear, Joaquin's attempt at saying hello or walking away because he was distracted. Since he didn't know Joaquin, he hadn't paid any attention to him.

"What's the matter, *mi amor*?" Cati asked as she sat with Joaquin, holding his hand and rubbing the top of his thumb with hers. Joaquin was silent, and she could tell he was not listening or aware of anyone or anything around him. He just kept a constant gaze at the ground. Cati placed her hand very softly on his face, pulled him out of his trance, and forced him to look at her. "We haven't seen or spoken to my *tio* in many years. I was so excited to show him the man I am with, but you seemed as if you didn't want to be there. What's wrong?"

Joaquin, not knowing where to begin or what he should say, asked her, "Cati, what does your *tio* do?"

She sat upright and seemed puzzled by his question. "What do you mean, what does he do?"

He responded, "Yes, do you have any idea who he is and what he does?"

She took a moment to answer, "What does that have anything to do with how you treated him when all he wanted to say was hello." Her tone revealed she was becoming irritated by Joaquin's questions.

"Can you please just answer me!" Joaquin begged. This caused Cati to pull her hands away from him. "Cati, he is not the man you all think he is. He is not a good man at all."

"How can you say these things about my *tio*; you don't even know him. He has always been there for my family and me, and he takes care of anyone who needs help. My *tio* manages many factories and is very important to his company. He has brought nothing but good to our area and has kept us all from need."

"Cati, *mi amor*, you may think that this is all he does, but he is much worse than that. He steals families and forces them to—" he started saying.

She interrupted Joaquin and yelled, "Just stop! I am not going to sit here and allow you to speak badly about a man who has taken care of us and helped so many people. I have known him my entire life. You are just meeting him for the first time, and you have the nerve to speak these bad things about him? I think you need to just go home." She stood up and began to walk away.

Joaquin tried to grab her arm to pull her back, but she pulled away and walked off. Not knowing what else to say or do, Joaquin headed back home. He knew it was a long way home, but he needed the time alone.

He was able to catch rides along the road until he reached the farm he had spent the last five years growing to love. Back in his little cottage, the face of that man kept appearing to him. Everywhere he turned, he would see that scarred face, and his anger grew more and more. The only thing that kept him from completely losing it was knowing he had upset Cati, and that made him sad. He never wanted to upset her. He kept thinking of ways to apologize to her; he just wanted to take back that moment. As he was going back and forth between being angry at seeing the man who killed his mother and feeling remorse for upsetting Cati, he noticed a set of headlights approaching. He figured Cati had come home to finish yelling at him. He was going to wait to apologize, let her come up to the cottage so that he didn't make a big scene in front of her parents.

He heard her walking up and decided he would meet her outside. Joaquin bolted out the door and began to say, "¡Mi amor! I'm so sor—" He was cut short when he felt something hit him on the back of the head. This caused him to fall face first onto the ground. He wasn't completely out, but very dazed. Joaquin tried to stand back up, but was met with another strike to his face, and he blacked out.

Moments after Joaquin had left the party and started making his way home, Cati went to look for her parents and found them with other family members. Cati's mother could sense something off and asked her what was wrong because Joaquin was no longer around. Cati began to cry and told her what happened. Her mother, astonished, looked at her husband. They both were trying to understand these accusations and why Joaquin would say such things.

So Cati's father went to confront his wife's brother with what he just learned. His main intention was to find out what happened to his son. They were hoping to finally see him there at the party, but when he didn't show up, they were concerned and needed to know. As Señor Hernandez approached his wife's brother, he was quickly stopped by an armed man.

"*Déjalo pasar*. That's *mi cuñado*. He isn't here to hurt me."

Cati's father removed his hat and came closer. "*Perdóname*, Lupe, I needed to ask you something. Have you seen my son, Pedro? He has not called or contacted us for a very long time, and we just wanted to know if you have seen or heard from him. We know you're a very busy man. I hope I'm not bothering you."

"Look at you, Chepe. If only you would've come to work with me when I asked, you wouldn't be standing there like a beggar needing money. You would be sitting here at this table with me. Instead, your son was smart enough to not be stuck on the farm, came with me, and now you ask me where he is? Well, to be honest, I thought he was here. I was told he'd be here." Lupe turned to his men, looking at them as if telling them to agree with him. They all nodded. "You see, Chepe, there's nothing else I know, and I can't help you. You can go back and sit with the rest of the people."

Cati's voice came from behind her father. "Wow, you have changed! Why are you being so dismissive of my father?" she questioned. "We just want to know where Pedro is."

"¡*Cállate*, Catalina! Be quiet," her father scolded. "*Perdóname*, Lupe, she's upset about not seeing her brother, and with the young man she came with."

"No, I'm upset that he doesn't seem to care that Pedro hasn't called or isn't even here. It has me wondering if those things that Joaquin said may be true!" Cati said angrily, causing Lupe to look up quickly.

"What did this Joaquin say?" Lupe said in a very interesting manner.

Joaquin woke up to the smell of cigarette smoke and beer. With his mind fuzzy from the hits to the head, he tried to focus on what was happening and where the smell was coming from. The two men guarding him poured a can of beer over his head to wake him up more. As they laughed, Joaquin realized he was tied to the chair and tried to break free, but fell over in the chair instead. This caused more laughter from the men, and one kicked dirt into his face, causing Joaquin to cough and spit dirt from his mouth.

A vehicle was approaching, and the men sat Joaquin back upright. As the vehicle stopped, it caused a cloud of dirt which made it difficult for Joaquin to see who exited the car. He did hear a scream that sounded like Cati.

"No! What are you doing to him? Let him go!"

As the cloud of dust cleared, Joaquin could see Cati and her parents inside the large SUV before the door was closed. Two other vehicles pulled up, causing another cloud of dust. Several men exited the vehicles and behind them, walking towards Joaquin, he saw the silhouette of a man. It was *El Guardián*. Once he stepped into the light, Joaquin could see him with a cigar in his mouth and a glass of something in his hand. He was taking a couple of slow sips as he walked up to the tied-up Joaquin. He then tossed the glass and took a long drag from his cigar. He blew the smoke into Joaquin's face, causing him to cough.

"So, I'm told you have something to tell me. I figured I'd give you the opportunity to tell me directly since you left my daughter's *quinceañera* so quickly." Joaquin shifted, trying to break free. "I really don't appreciate people starting or spreading rumors about me. Especially ones who say I'm a bad person. With everything that I do for this family and the people in the town, how can anyone say I'm a bad person?" he asked, standing with his arms open as if to hug the whole town and everything around him.

Joaquin answered, "I've seen how you treat people, and I know for a fact you're a liar!"

Lupe put his hands down and balled up his fists because he did not like to be called a liar. "You're speaking pretty bravely for someone who wants to have a life with my *sobrina*. Where do you get off, accusing me of such things?"

"Untie me and let's find out!" Joaquin shouted back. "Maybe I'll finish what I started and make the other side of your face match, Guardian!"

Confusion stopped Lupe at first; then he realized this was the boy who hit him in the face with a stick long ago. He didn't recognize him because the last time he'd seen him Joaquin was very small for his age, and he was covered in blood and surrounded by vultures. "Well, you have certainly grown up, haven't you? I guess working on this farm was what you needed to get some weight on you," he said mockingly.

Lupe looked at his men. "This is the little shit—well, not so little anymore—that gave me my good looks years ago," he said, showing off his face with the scars. "I had to sacrifice my own *sobrino* because of this *pendejo*. When the *federales* came through, I would have gotten away sooner, but I was busy watching the vultures eat at this little fucker's face. I had to use Pedro as a shield so they didn't shoot me. Oh well, he's gone now." The men started giggling at what Lupe said.

He then turned back to Joaquin and asked, "How is your mother, by the way; did she come along with you? I would love to fuck her a few more times. I could have my choice of holes, but I think I'll choose one of the two holes in her forehead."

The rope holding Joaquin was tearing into his skin because of how hard he was trying to break free. Hearing Cati's uncle speak of Joaquin's mother that way made him rage with hate, and he tried to break free, only to fall again.

The warden laughed at Joaquin's falling, kicked him in the stomach, and spit on him. Then, as if a completely different person, he lunged close to Joaquin's face and screamed, "NO ONE SPREADS BAD THINGS ABOUT ME, DAMMIT! NO ONE!"

"Take this *hijo de puta* outta my face," he tells his men in a calm manner. "I have a special place to deal with him. Plus, I wouldn't want *mi familia* to think I was a bad man, now would I?"

They picked Joaquin off the ground, untied him from the chair, and tied his hands behind his back. Then, they tossed him in the back of one of the SUVs. Before leaving, they let Cati and her parents out and told them that, if they spoke of any of this to anyone, they would be back. As they left, Joaquin saw the red and amber flames sweep through the fields. He was kicking and screaming, hoping that no harm would come to Cati and her parents.

"*Tranquilo, pendejo*, we're not going to harm them. That's his family. We just burned their fields as punishment and to show them we mean what we said about not telling anyone."

Joaquin wanted to believe them, but with everything he had witnessed, he just couldn't trust what they said. He had to make sure they were all right, but he was tied up and had no way of getting to them. Breaking free right now would only put them in more danger because the men could easily turn around and chase him back to the farm. He needed to have a plan and figure out how and when he could escape.

These men clearly didn't know how to tie a rope very well, because, once Joaquin relaxed a moment to think, he realized that he could easily slip from the binding. A mixture of sweat and blood on his hands gave his skin enough lubrication to be able to pull free of the ropes. He knew he had plenty of time to think of a plan. The place that the warden was referring to was at least five hours away, and they would have to stop eventually to urinate. The place they were taking Joaquin to was deep in the jungles of Lacandon and one of many places they took people to get rid of.

After about three hours of driving Joaquin noticed they began to slow down. Eventually they came to a stop, and one by one they exited their vehicles and relieved themselves. There was some miscommunication amongst the men in the vehicle with Joaquin because they all jumped out almost immediately at the same time. That was the chance Joaquin was waiting for.

He slipped one hand free from the ropes and looked around to see where the men were. The two other vehicles were still a good few hundred feet away from them, and the men that were in his vehicle were all facing away from him. With his hands free, he braced himself and kicked at the window opposite of where the men were standing. It cracked, and Joaquin looked to be sure that they hadn't heard anything. Seeing no reaction from them, he kicked the window again, and this time it fell out in one piece. The bubbled-up tint held it together, so it didn't shatter. The noise it made when it fell, however, did get their attention.

The men scrambled to zip their pants and quickly ran to their vehicles. By the time they got back to the car, Joaquin had vanished. The place they chose to stop was very close to the wooded jungle, so he was able to escape through there. Phone calls were made. Within no time, more jeeps and dirt bikes arrived, and several men made their way into the jungle in search of Joaquin.

Joaquin had a good hour and a half on them. It was a very hot day, and his clothes were already soaked and sticking to his body. He hadn't stopped running, and his muscles were beginning to cramp from heat exhaustion and thirst. He needed to find water, but didn't want to waste time getting caught over water. His body decided to make the decision for him.

His right leg muscle tightened up, and Joaquin tripped and fell down a lower cliff he was running alongside. The cliff wasn't steep, but it was a long way down. He tried to stop himself from tumbling and sliding, but the momentum was too much. He finally came to a stop and, thankfully, there wasn't anything from his tumble that would cause serious injuries. He lay there for a moment to catch his breath, get his bearings, and mentally feel if anything was hurt or broken. Just a few minor scrapes and dirt everywhere was all he could feel. He quickly sat up, looked around, and noticed a creek. The water he needed!

Joaquin took a moment, hydrated himself, and decided to keep going. He was unsure where, but he knew he couldn't stop until he felt he was far away from that place. He decided to keep moving upstream with the creek and, hopefully, find a pueblo.

It started to get dark after many hours of searching. The men on bikes and jeeps searched everywhere. They almost stopped looking until they found the trail where Joaquin had fallen off the cliff. They sped down to the creek bed and began following the trail up creek. The lead biker suddenly came to a stop. After crossing through a long clearing, the creek seemed to disappear into the woods. Everyone else behind him stopped.

The lead biker dropped his bike and ran up to the edge of the wooded area. He noticed a particular stone carving with ancient lettering. Directly next to that, a long spike and a skull wrapped with leather, feathers, and smaller bones. The man immediately began to shake and speak in a Native language. He grabbed the cross from his necklace, kissed it, jumped back on his bike, and sped off in the opposite direction.

The warden's men were puzzled and had no idea what just happened. They just knew that they needed to go after Joaquin and bring him back, or suffer the consequences.

Chapter 6

The Knife

"Okay, let's go, you guys, off the bus!" an officer yelled out. Joaquin notices the uniforms of the men where they stopped. Maverick County. The ones wearing the red uniforms in the front of the bus stand up and start getting off. Those were then replaced with other men wearing red-and-orange uniforms. The other passengers on the bus seemed confused at what was going on, but Joaquin had been here before. Those first set of men whom they picked up were just picked up to be brought to this facility so they could be taken to a nearby holding facility to await court dates. The new men would be taken to the next facility, typically for the same purpose. Many times, one facility doesn't have the bed space to hold all the men in their jurisdiction, so the detainees are taken to whatever facility has room.

Once the new passengers were seated, the officers from the facility came to the bus with several large boxes. They contained lunch for the men on the buses. The officers started handing out the Styrofoam trays to each of the men. It was a bit difficult to eat with their hands tied to their waists, but they managed. Joaquin had not eaten breakfast, so he was pretty hungry. He opened the tray and found two hot dogs and chips with a cookie. The officers then came back and handed out water. The men on the bus were relieved to have food and also thirsty from the long ride thus far. After about twenty minutes or so, the officers came back with trash bags and picked up what was left. The men who still had food left over either gave it to others who wanted more or kept it for later during the ride. They were unsure how long the ride was going to be, and they didn't want to go hungry.

Shortly after eating, the officers started allowing the men to use the bathroom at the back of the bus. There was only one toilet, so the process took some time. By the time it was Joaquin's turn, he really needed to go. Once inside the small toilet area, he felt a little claustrophobic. He just quickly did his business and got out.

The bus was on the road again after all was settled and everyone accounted for. It took a while for Joaquin to shake that feeling of being closed in. His breathing sped up, and his heart was racing. He sat down and tried to let the feeling pass.

After seeing that first biker in so much fear, it started a chain reaction through the other riders. They would run up to what he saw and run back to their bikes, all saying the same chant and holding on to different medallions around their necks. They got back on their bikes very frightened and sped off. This upset the warden's men because they were hired to help find Joaquin, but they were running away.

"Where the fuck are those *hijo de putas* going?" one of the warden's men asked.

They managed to stop a biker from speeding off, and they couldn't understand a word he was saying. One of the armed men with them understood and said, "They are frightened because apparently we have come across an ancient tribe that was thought to be lost for many years."

"Well then, why did they run away? We have plenty of guns, and we can't go back without that fucker, or we'll be the ones filling that ditch."

"You don't understand; those are ancient writings, and they said only death leads this way. It was put there to keep people away. I'm still not sure of everything they said, but they won't go any further."

"Fine, he doesn't want to go any further, then he doesn't have to."

That armed man took out his sidearm and pointed it at the head of the scared biker, who kept chanting something in that native tongue. The biker then looked at him, eyes filled with tears, and said *gracias* in a soft voice. He then grabbed the armed man's gun hand and squeezed the trigger, holding the gun to his own head.

Blood and brain spattered all over the man who was interpreting. He began to vomit when he realized pieces of brain had gotten into his opened mouth and blood was running down his face. The other armed men began to question whether it was a good idea to pursue Joaquin into that place. They mentioned how those bikers who lived in this area were afraid and didn't want to go in there, so maybe they should reconsider.

The one leading them scolded, "*Mira, pendejos,* you already know what will happen if we don't have that *pinche cabrón* where the warden wants him. So you either stop your crying, or end up like this *puto* here." With that, they loaded into their Jeeps and proceeded into that section of the forest.

After following the creek for what seemed like several hours, the creek appeared to stop at a large boulder. From there, there was only one small path that you could tell was a walking path. The trees were not so thick, but Joaquin could only see so far in the moonlight. He decided that it was too dark to travel without being able to see. Around the big boulder, he found an area that was covered, and he decided to stay for the night.

He made himself as comfortable as possible and was trying to relax. His breathing started slowing down after running for so long, and he was able to finally hear the sounds of the forest. The night animals were starting to wake as the day creatures found their places to rest. The sounds of the trees creaking from the wind made it seem as if they were alive and moving around.

He was unsure how long he'd stayed there or how long he'd slept, but the sunlight beaming through the trees awakened him. He looked around and saw no one, but he did hear some voices. He slowly and quietly looked to be sure it wasn't the men who were pursuing him. When he saw it was not they, but some women and children filling up basins of water, he felt relieved and approached them.

Joaquin noticed that they were wearing what seemed to be old native clothing, rather than the regular clothes he was accustomed to seeing. The boys had on what seemed to be leather loincloths, and their hair was cut as if a bowl had been placed on top of their heads. The women wore only long leather skirts with beaded necklaces. Either their hair was braided, or it was just left undone and covering their chests. He noticed that their skin seemed to have been painted with a red color of some sort. When they saw Joaquin coming nearer, they began to scream and run.

Joaquin put his hands up and pleaded for their help, but no one stopped to listen. He started running in the direction that they were headed, but he didn't make it far before feeling something poke his chest. He looked down to see a dart. Two others found their mark as one hit his arm and the other his forehead. Before he fell to the ground he looked into the woods and saw a figure holding something to his mouth. He fell facedown but was still awake. Because he couldn't move any of his limbs or speak, he was moving his eyes in an effort to see what was happening.

Joaquin was met with dirty, bare feet in his line of sight before he was pushed over; then, he saw the men who had him. Two of the men carried the long, hollow shafts that were used for the darts. They wore similar clothing as the young boys, but the men had some sort of piercings that appeared to be bones going through their lips and cheeks. One of them wore a necklace with several longer pieces of bone on it. It was becoming difficult to see as Joaquin's vision was going blurry.

They began speaking in a language Joaquin didn't understand at first, but realized that a few of the words here and there were similar to some words his mother would say. He had never heard anyone else speak those words, so he figured they were words his mother made up just for him. He tried to understand, but they were speaking too fast, and he hadn't heard those words for such a long time. He did understand one word, *blood*, as it was said several times. *Good* and *food*, then *take*—those were the only other words he was able to make out before he was dragged away by his feet.

He just lay helpless as they dragged him along the path, over stones and anything else that was on the ground. Though he was unable to move, he was able to feel every rock and stick he hit. The scraping of his skin hurt so much as the blood mixed in with dirt built up more and more at the back of his head. His arms up over his head as they dragged him did not help prevent damage to his body. They walked for what seemed like three miles before they came to a stop. Other men, yelling in their native tongue, came running with similar hollow rods. This prompted the men dragging Joaquin to let him go and leave with the twenty or so other men.

Joaquin lay there unable to move, his arms over his head. He heard some footsteps approaching quietly. Moving his eyes, he was able to glance at who was there—a younger man with a few other boys his age. They were curious as to who he was and slowly and cautiously approached him. Once the young man was close, he poked Joaquin and then did it again, trying to get a reaction out of him. When he didn't react or move, that young man started reaching into Joaquin's pockets, looking for anything he could find. He came up empty. The boy patted Joaquin all along his legs, and then he reached inside the waistband of Joaquin's pants. That's when he found where Joaquin had hidden his father's pocketknife. It was in a leather sheath just inside the beltline. The armed men had missed it when they searched him, but Joaquin couldn't reach it with his hands tied behind his back. The young man took the pocketknife out to inspect it, said something, and then ran off with it. Joaquin tried to yell for him, but only grunts and inside screams came out, and the young man did not stop or turn. He simply disappeared into the forest.

Joaquin was lying there, hoping he could regain some feeling, when he heard gunfire. Many shots came from the direction the native men had run. Then, as quickly as it started, the gunshots stopped. A short while later, not as many men appeared on the trail. The men who did show were dragging other men behind them. Joaquin couldn't make out who it was from the angle he was lying, but he assumed it had to be the armed men who were chasing him. Once the natives reached Joaquin, they grabbed him and once again started pulling him by his feet. Chants and yelling echoed in the forest as the men walked on with their victory trophies.

Before getting to the village, the men became extremely silent and no longer chanted or made any type of noise. Even the sound of their breathing almost stopped, despite dragging the men and walking such a long distance. Joaquin was gaining some feeling back and was able to move his head enough to see people along the pathway; they were just staring without any expression. Many grass huts with people standing in the doorways was all that he could see. They passed a larger hut that didn't appear lived in, but it could hold a bunch of people. An area just past all the huts had cages made from bamboo and sticks.

The ground became wet and soft as they passed one area. Joaquin saw that the men's feet were red after stepping in the softer area. He looked and noticed that the ground leading to a large stone was a dark-crimson color. He figured that was what was causing the men's feet to turn red. The native men started tying up all the captured men. One by one, by their hands, they strung them up from the tops of those cages. Joaquin was the first one to be hung, and he was able to watch as the other five were pulled by their hands into the air. He also saw a large group of the villagers gather around but not say a word or make any noise.

They took their time on the last one as they stripped him naked and covered him in the red dirt. They tied a stick between his ankles to keep his legs spread and pulled him up in the cage upside-down. By this time, Joaquin had regained most of his feeling and tried to shake free, but was unable to. He heard some muffled cries coming from the other men as they still didn't have much feeling back. Once the man who was tied upside-down was secured, one of the natives drew out a knife and slowly walked over to him.

Joaquin watched as the remainder of the people stood in complete silence; no one blinked or made a sound. Then, as if they all knew at the same time, just before the knife-holding native continued, the entire group hissed and gave a long sigh with their eyes opened as wide as they could go and their tongues hanging out. At the end of the first sigh, with a single motion, the native with the knife sliced the hanging man's belly just below the sternum. The hanging man opened his eyes, but was unable to scream or make any noise. Joaquin could tell that he felt the blade go through his skin, and with the amount of pain it must have caused, the hanging man's body jerked back and forth.

The native then held up his hand, which was empty. That caused another round of hissing and sighing in unison. Again at the end of the first sigh, into the open cut, the native rammed his hand as deep as it could go, as if he was searching for something specific. Blood started pouring out of the hanging body as the native found what he was looking for and began pulling. He continued to withdraw his arm from the cavity, until what he had been seeking was exposed but not free. With the knife in his other hand, the native began cutting. After the first cut, a large spray of blood covered his face and chest. It only took a couple more slices before Joaquin could see exactly what he was cutting out. The native held up high the heart of the defense-less man and showed it to the crowd before him. The hissing and sighing stopped immediately as the heart came into view. After only a few pumps, the heart stopped moving, and the native took it, put as much as he could fit into his mouth, and bit into it. He chewed it slowly, as if savoring it.

The native only chewed for a moment before making a disgusted look and spitting out the heart. This caused the group to start chanting "Hah, hah, hah!" over and over as they lowered that man and dragged him to a ditch. They threw him in the ditch as if throwing out unwanted garbage.

The next man in line was lowered. By this time, the men had started to regain feeling and were able to attempt to break free and to scream and yell. He was stripped naked and tied the same way as the previous man. The group of onlookers remained quiet until their cue to hiss and sigh. The native with the knife repeated the same procedure to obtain the heart. This time after eating it, he swallowed and threw the heart into the crowd. There was a little scuffle for the prize, but it was done in silence, and it was quickly divided by a few people. One of the men gave his younger child a small piece of it, and the child gladly ate it without hesitation. They then lowered the hanging man and carried him to that larger hut.

The remaining men hung there in complete shock at what they'd just witnessed. They realized that they would not be leaving this village. Crowds of villagers lined up outside the large hut, as if patiently waiting. Then, one at a time, they received a piece of the man, and the villagers went back to their own huts and prepared dinner for their families. The men hanging were struggling and trying to break free, but couldn't and only exhausted themselves instead. Joaquin tried a few times to free himself and realized that there was no escaping. Just as the sun was almost down, the men were lowered just enough so that they could sit on the ground, but still with their hands above them. The tied-up men tried to stand up and free themselves somehow, but were pulled by the ropes holding them. They realized that as long as they stayed sitting down with their arms above them, they would not be pulled up.

Joaquin, still shocked and scared of what was happening, didn't try escaping anymore after being pulled up twice. He just stayed there and tried to figure out what was going to happen and how much longer he had. He sat there as the night air grew chilly on his back, which was exposed from being dragged through that wet red mud. The natives left two of their men to stand watch in case one of the captives attempted to escape. Joaquin began thinking of Cati and how he was taken from her. He missed her so much and just wanted to see her smile again. He longed for her touch and the soft kisses she would give him on his forehead when they lay together. He then prayed that they were all okay and that he would one day meet them again, either in this life or the next.

The next morning came, and the men, who hadn't slept at all for fear of what could happen, were brought water and food containing fruits and beans with some *tortillas de maíz*. Joaquin was surprised at this after witnessing the horrendous ritual the day prior. They weren't given much time to eat, and most of the men refused to eat, not knowing what it was made from. Joaquin decided to at least have some water and eat the fruit. They were then pulled up to hang again, as when they first arrived. The two guards left, and the men stayed there alone, hanging. This went on for the next few days, from what Joaquin could gather. Then, the man, who had done that ritual the first day, came back out and performed once again.

The hanging men begged and pleaded and tried more and more to be freed. It was no use, since the natives didn't understand them, and they seemed not to be moved by their cries for help. The next man up almost broke free when they were getting him naked, but he was knocked unconscious by another native standing close-by with a club of some sort. Not knowing the customs or rituals made Joaquin uncertain of when he might die. The hissing and sighing broke Joaquin's train of thought, and he saw the man holding the knife eat the heart and throw the rest into the crowd. This man was accepted, carried out, and divided amongst the village. That left only two more men before it was Joaquin's turn to see if he was worthy to be shared with the village.

Three more days passed and the next man had already accepted his fate and didn't fight at all. He was crying and praying for his family. Once they had him upside-down, he couldn't hold his bodily fluids, and he urinated on himself. This seemed to upset the native with the knife, and he took the man's penis and cut it off. Blood began pouring from that wound, all over the hanging man, and it covered his body and face. The pain was so excruciating it caused him to pass out after the first initial scream while getting his penis cut off. The native continued with the ritual, and he was accepted.

The stress of knowing you're going to die is terrible. Seeing how you're going to die is even worse. The two remaining men had nowhere to go and no way of escape, except by being cut into even parts for a village to enjoy.

Two days later, Joaquin had refused his meal as he didn't see the point of eating only to be eaten by the village. He simply no longer cared to wait to see when he was next to die. The young man who had taken his knife was being pulled by the neck of an older man as if telling him to lead him. Once they got to the cage, the young man pointed at Joaquin, and there were a few words exchanged. The older man looked at Joaquin with a cold, dead stare.

What does this mean? What is going on? was all that Joaquin could think.

The older man released the younger man's neck and pushed him away, as if to say go, then ordered Joaquin to be lowered. This confused Joaquin because it was only the second day since the last feeding, and he was not next to have his heart ripped out while he was still alive. Either way, he had accepted his fate and didn't put up much of a fight. With his hands still bound in front of him, the older native pulled Joaquin and quickly headed away from the village. Joaquin was having a difficult time keeping up since he had been suspended in the air for the better part of a week, and he hadn't eaten much either. That didn't stop the native from pulling Joaquin with urgency and leading him just up the hill, at times dragging him as Joaquin would trip or would not be able to keep up. Joaquin tried to regain his footing, but the man didn't stop and just kept pulling and pushing him until they reached a single hut. From this hut, the rest of the village was visible, and Joaquin could see the cage he had been kept in.

The man who escorted Joaquin pointed to the hut, grunted, motioned with his hand, and said a word in his native tongue that Joaquin understood to be "GO." His mother would say this to him from time to time when she wanted him to leave the room or go take a bath.

Joaquin complied with the demand and walked towards the hut. When he looked back over his shoulder, the man who escorted him was gone. Joaquin turned around to see where he might have gone, but there was no trace in any direction. When he turned back around, Joaquin was frightened by someone standing in front of him. The last thing he remembered seeing was someone with black-painted skin, red eyes, no teeth, and long, dirty hair dripping with blood. The figure before him blew a powder into his face, which made Joaquin disoriented and gave him blurred vision.

Joaquin woke up and found himself on a table covered with spurts of blood. He looked around, didn't see anyone around, and quickly checked his body. No wounds. He stood up from the table and noticed on a small table next to him a small dead animal of some sort. He couldn't make it out because it was cut up. He figured that is where the blood came from. The dead animal was in a bowl that had old bones tossed on top of it. There were a few burning candles there, as well as the knife that belonged to his father. Looking around more closely, just placed on different tables all over, he noticed many skulls of different animals. Then, he saw a trail of bones leading to a large chair made of more bones, and it had human skulls all along the high top and on the armrest. The room had a certain chill that he couldn't explain since it was the warm season and there was a fire going.

Then, as though a cold draft had come through, he heard the words, *"¿Quién eres tú?"* The sound was low and firm, but a bit raspy. This startled Joaquin because he hadn't heard anyone speaking in Spanish in the village, and he couldn't see anyone or tell from where the voice was coming.

"Who are you?" the voice asked again.

This time, Joaquin saw a dark figure move on one side of the hut, but couldn't see any features because it stayed in the shadows. *"Me llamo Joaquin Navarez,"* he answered in a shaky tone. He kept looking around, hoping to see with whom he was speaking, but only saw moving shadows. Joaquin was afraid to move because by now he realized where he was and didn't want to upset the *curandero*.

"Why are you here?" the voice asked.

"I didn't mean to come here. I was running from those other men that were captured," Joaquin replied.

"¡¡MENTIRAS!!" the voice yelled.

It sounded as if it was coming from right next to him, and when Joaquin turned, he felt a strike to his face. It caused Joaquin to fall to his knees. When he went to get up, the curandero was standing right in his face. His skin was leatherlike, and he had a single tooth you could see when he spoke. His skin was painted black and his eyelids red. Joaquin could see that his hair was long and crusted from that mud by the cages. He had bone piercings through the bridge of his nose and his septum. His skin had many scars in a specific pattern along his chest. He wore a similar loincloth as the other villagers, but after seeing it up close, he noticed it was not leather from animals. He then saw a drape over his shoulders that appeared to be woven human hair.

"You're here to run us out, like everyone else that has tried for centuries. Now, tell me, what do you want?"

Joaquin took a step back and put his head down so as to not look the *curandero* in the eyes. "I'm telling you the truth. These men tried to kill me, and I escaped, and they chased me into this jungle."

The *curandero* looked at Joaquin for a second and then asked, "Where did you steal that knife from?"

"That knife belonged to my father, and his father before him, and his father before him. It is the only thing I have of my father before he was killed by men like those that are after me," Joaquin told him.

The *curandero* raised his hand to strike Joaquin, but when he saw Joaquin did not move or flinch, he knew he was telling the truth, so he put his hand down.

"I may have done many questionable things and have done things wrong, but I am no liar," he proudly stated while looking the *curandero* in the eyes.

"Yes, I know you are telling the truth. The powder that I blew in your face wouldn't allow you to lie to me," the *curandero* said.

Just as they were speaking, Joaquin could hear a commotion from the village, the next feeding ceremony was getting ready to start. The hut had no windows, so he hadn't realized that he had been there an entire day. They could hear the screams and yelling from the last remaining man in the cage.

The *curandero* invited Joaquin outside to watch. "I enjoy watching the ceremony."

Joaquin followed him slowly, uncertain what was going on. Minutes ago, he was sure he was going to die, but now he felt like a guest and a spectator at a *fútbol* game.

"What is so special about that knife?" Joaquin asked.

"When I was a young boy, I would wander off in the jungle, even though my father told me not to. I came across some men with guns, and when they saw me, they began shooting at me. Not the guns that these men had but those long ones that only shot one at a time. I started running, but one of the bullets hit me in my leg. They captured me and took me back to where they were. I was in that camp for many months, and I was able to pick up the language a little bit. A younger boy who was working with the horses saw me and knew I was not like them. He was about my age as well, and he would bring me food secretly. One evening, a battle happened at the camp, and everything was burning, and many people were dying. I was trapped in this cage they had, and that young boy released me and showed me the way out of the camp area. He followed me back to where they found me; then the boy told me to go. Before I left, I gave him the knife I had that my father gave me. It was too small to be a threat to the men; that's why they didn't take it."

Joaquin stood there in amazement at the story he was just told. It almost seemed too farfetched because that would mean that the *curandero* was over a hundred years old. He didn't appear to be that age, but Joaquin would hear stories of long-ago natives living to two hundred years because they didn't live in the modern times like everyone else. Joaquin's amazement was interrupted by the hissing of the natives. He looked at the crowd as there was more hissing and then "hah, hah, hah." The native who was performing the ceremony spit out the heart he'd bitten into.

El curandero said, *"Tienes que irte ahora."* You need to go now. That's all he said, and then he reached for Joaquin.

Joaquin didn't hear the urgency in the *curandero*'s voice because, after the native who was performing the ceremony spit out the heart, it was as if Joaquin could see his eyes looking right at him from all the way down where he was. Those piercing eyes were glued to Joaquin and the native pointed with his knife in Joaquin's direction. The body of the hanging man was tossed into the ditch along with the others, and a few men were headed up the trail that led to where Joaquin was.

"You must leave now!" the *curandero* yelled this time. Pulling Joaquin, he led him to another trail behind his hut.

"What's going on? What's wrong?" Joaquin asked as they were almost running.

"No one is allowed to leave once they've been here, and since you were next in line, they will come for you. I am repaying my debt to you and your family as it was once done for me. Now you must run, and don't stop until you come to a crossing. Keep running to the right, and don't you stop until you jump off the cliff." The *curandero* stopped as he was out of breath and could no longer run.

Joaquin looked past him and saw those men as they arrived at the hut. They then looked in their direction and began running. That prompted Joaquin to run and not stop. He was unsure how far he needed to run, but he kept going. Soon, he wished he had eaten the last meals he was offered because he started slowing down and was becoming tired. The men chasing him did not seem to tire as they were getting closer by each step. Joaquin finally came to the crossing in the road. He turned right and kept running as fast and as hard as he could.

He turned to look and saw the men getting closer. One was twirling a bolas over his head, and another had a long rod pressed against his mouth. The one twirling the bolas let it go, and it wrapped around one of Joaquin's legs. It almost grabbed the other leg, but he had jumped at the perfect time, so it didn't catch him. Then he felt a dart wiz past his face. He had to keep going and tried to go faster, but with the bolas on his leg he wasn't able to pick up speed.

Finally he saw the cliff. It took him a moment to consider stopping before he jumped since he had no idea what he was jumping into or how far down it was. It could've been a ditch with spikes or just a tall cliff with rocks at the bottom. He had no way of knowing. The only thing he knew was that he did not want to die seeing his heart pulled from his body. After quickly considering his options, Joaquin didn't even think about it before he jumped as far as he could over that cliff into a cloudy mist.

Chapter 7

Lost

Joaquin never really figured himself to be adventurous or, as some would say, a thrill seeker. He only wanted to make it to America and live a quiet life with a wife and children. Even with everything he had gone through, he never saw himself better than anyone or considered himself less fortunate. Talking about what he had to endure to get to America was something someone seeking pity would do, he thought. Joaquin did not want anyone to feel pity for him. He went through what he went through for a reason, and he just accepted whatever challenges came his way and relied on Dios to help him through it.

On this long two-lane road to their next heavily guarded gate, Joaquin couldn't help but say a prayer for the *curandero* who helped him escape. He couldn't be more thankful that he let him go just because his great-grandfather helped him a long time ago. Although, he might have enjoyed feasting on him if they had been able to capture him. Then Joaquin thought to himself, *Well, that explains why the handle always looked like a bone.*

Wilbur, who was sitting next to him, interrupted his thoughts, "*¿Entonces, a dónde vas?*"

Joaquin answered, "They're supposed to deport me. This is my second time. I just hope they don't send me to Honduras. The first time I was able to convince them I was from Mexico, but I'm not so sure this time."

"*Sí,* I tried telling them I was from Mexico too so that I don't have to go so far coming back." They both chuckled a little.

Joaquin wasn't one to lie, but to go back to Honduras was especially devastating for most people since it meant they had to start all over on their journey to America. For Joaquin, it was even more difficult because, as far as he knew, he didn't have any family in Honduras. Going back there would just be a constant reminder of his mother, and being haunted by her murder was something he could not endure.

For a while, the two of them spoke back and forth about how they'd been treated after being caught. For the most part, they agreed that, though things would have been much better had they not been caught, and even though they weren't anticipating getting caught, it wasn't nearly as bad as what they would have had to live through there in Mexico or Honduras.

Wilbur continued talking about politics in Mexico, and those conversations never interested Joaquin, so he started thinking about anything else he could to escape the conversation. He wasn't trying to be rude, but having to choose between talking about the politics of the world and Mexico, or being tied up and having his heart ripped from his chest, seemed like an easy decision.

The jump over the cliff was gut-wrenching. Joaquin couldn't see what he was jumping into or where he would land, and the fall was even worse. The fall seemed as though it wouldn't end; he only wished he could see where he was falling. Finally, the mist began to clear, and he could see what was waiting for him.

When he hit the water, the air was immediately pushed out of him, and if Joaquin hadn't been holding himself straight like a board, his spine and every bone in his body might have broken. Even to this day, he wasn't sure how he survived that fall, but at his current his age, he could feel the effects of it. He had to hurry and get back to the surface since all the air had been taken from him. On his way up, he felt as though he swallowed half of the pool he was in. The surface seems so far away when you're fighting for your life to breathe and not take in all that water. Coming up for that breath of air almost felt as if it were his very first, like a birth. Coughing and choking followed as he was trying to breathe and stop sucking down all the water around him.

Another giant splash came just a few moments after he came up for air, and then another. This scared Joaquin, and he tried to swim as fast as he could away from the splashes. From one of those splashes, he saw a body float to the top with its head facedown and blood turning the water red. That native appeared lifeless, so Joaquin didn't worry about him. Joaquin couldn't see a second body, so he looked around frantically. When he saw no one else, Joaquin decided he needed to get out of the water fast.

He started for a small bank close to where he was, but felt a strong pull on the collar of his shirt. An arm pulled him back into the water with several punches to his face and head. Joaquin was able to turn and kick free for a moment, but was grabbed again by the neck and pulled farther underwater. Joaquin wasn't able to get a full breath when he'd surfaced, so he couldn't hold his breath for very long. He was kicking and pulling as hard as he could, trying to free himself from being drowned. No matter how hard he struggled, Joaquin was powerless against the native holding him under the water, and he couldn't pull away.

Just then, he remembered his father's knife that he took back from the *curandero*. He was beginning to fade and only had one opportunity to free himself; he needed to do it quickly. He managed to retrieve the knife from inside his waistband and stabbed the knife as hard as he could into the man's leg several times. The native only let out the air he was holding in his lungs, but not Joaquin's neck. It actually made him squeeze harder around Joaquin's neck; the last and final attempt needed to count; otherwise, he would die.

Joaquin turned the knife around in his hand and, as hard as he could, used the knife as if he were trying to scratch the top side of his back. The knife found its target right above the native's ear. That is what it took to feel the grip around his neck loosen. Joaquin tried to pull his hand back with the knife, but it was difficult to pull out. It took a couple of tries until it slid out and blood began pouring from that wound. The man floated motionless in the water, his eyes open and staring into a blank, endless eternity.

Coughing and catching his breath again, Joaquin managed to get to the bank, where he crawled out as if using his last remaining ounce of energy. After a moment of rest, he looked at the pool he had landed in and then back up. With the fog in the way, he was unable to see his jumping-off point, but he could only imagine how high that jump was. There was a waterfall coming from the side of the rock formation that was creating the pool, and it led to a tunnel made from erosion. Joaquin stood up and walked around wondering how he was going to get out of this pool. The rock wall surrounding him was too high to climb, and there was no stream or river leading out of it. He came to one end that looked like a small cave under the rock formation. He didn't see how that could be a way out until he noticed a few leaves on top of the water; they were floating towards that small cave and disappearing. Joaquin was unsure if wading into the cave would be a good idea, not knowing if the water was too deep or if there was a way out through the cave.

Before he could even consider making another walk-through in case he had missed something, two more big splashes hit the water, and both men made it through. These men were bigger than the first two who had come down. They swam to their already deceased friends and did not appear happy to see them that way. They looked around in search of Joaquin. Thankfully he was out of their sight for the moment as they hadn't looked in his direction. He had no time to waste. He didn't know where to go or if he could fight these men off. He made the decision to take his chances and see if he could make it through like those leaves.

He dove in and headed for the cave. It didn't take much energy swimming, because as he got closer, the current picked up, and it took him in that direction. There was no turning back now as he disappeared into the cave, and it pulled him quickly through the tunnel. He had difficulty seeing after entering the cave because the sunlight was swallowed up by the darkness. Only the echo of the water and his coughing and splashing bounced off the walls as he was being carried by the current. Every so often, a natural window in the rock formation allowed a small bit of light into the tunnel, but it was quickly taken away, and Joaquin just prayed and hoped his ride would end soon.

Shortly thereafter, the rays of sunlight started to become more frequent, and he could smell moss and mildew. Then he saw a large opening ahead, and the water level quickly dropped. He was able to stand, as the water was only knee-high, and he swiftly made his way to the opening that he hoped led out the other side of the cave. With all the adrenaline running through him, Joaquin hadn't noticed how cold the water was, and when he made it to the opening of the tunnel, a chill came over him. The temperature inside that tunnel had to have been at least sixty-five degrees. Once he got to the opening, he quietly and safely looked around to see if there was anyone there who could potentially hurt him. The water from that tunnel poured into a creek that led away into the open jungle. The rocks leading away from the tunnel were soft and smooth from the erosion.

After he was clear of the tunnel and out of the water, Joaquin noticed the temperature quickly go back up, and he was no longer cold. With that heat, he knew he would quickly dry off. There was a path he found which led through the jungle, so he decided to stay on it until he saw any dangers. You could tell this path wasn't used much as you could barely see it, but coming out of the tunnel, it was fairly well visible. With his knife in his hand, he set out before it turned too dark to see where he was going.

Joaquin kept walking for the better part of a few hours, only stopping and resting when his muscles were beginning to cramp from the heat. He wasn't sure where he was going or what he would encounter on this path, but he just needed to get away from where he was. The day started to turn to night, and Joaquin was still nowhere near any sign of life besides the always-present monkeys throwing poop at him when he crossed into their territory. He was hit a couple of times, and that smell would never leave his nose because it was so pungent and the worst smell he had ever encountered.

With only a few minutes of daylight remaining, Joaquin was struggling to walk any farther. He was starting to become dizzy, and he couldn't remember when he stopped sweating. Also, he had lost track of the path a couple of hours before and was just walking away from where the sun was going down. He finally noticed a clearing ahead and was struggling to stay standing and walk without falling. When he reached that clearing, he could no longer continue. He attempted to lean up against a tree and rest a moment, but when it fell under his weight, he looked and realized it was a fence. The fall completely drained him, and he could no longer move. He then heard a dog barking in the distance. It reached him, and the last thing Joaquin saw was a dog standing over him, smelling him, and licking his face.

Several days went by, and Joaquin was just starting to come to; he tried moving, but having been so dehydrated, his muscles wouldn't cooperate. His lips were severely dry and cracked, and his throat scratchy and sore. His eyes were very dry and sensitive to the sunlight, but he needed to be sure that he wasn't back at that village. He appeared to be in a modern bedroom, and he was in a bed, so he was relieved about that for the moment.

Just then, the door opened, and a dog came to his face and began licking him again. Then a male voice said, "Hey, *Chucho*! Ya! *¡Déjalo en paz!*" The dog took its final lick and backed away. "I'm sorry; he gets excited when new people are around. He's always so friendly, and he's supposed to be the guard dog. He doesn't do that good of a job, as you can tell. Although he does growl at my brother's mother-in-law. She's a *bruja*, if you know what I mean. " He swatted the dog away and sat next to Joaquin in a chair by the bed.

Joaquin, unable to speak, tried to sit up and make any noise with his mouth in an attempt to communicate.

"No, no, it's okay; don't try and talk. You're very dehydrated, and you need to rest. I'm just happy you woke up. I was getting worried you wouldn't. Plus, it gets a little weird when you're talking with someone, and they don't answer you back. Somebody might think I'm crazy for talking to myself," he told Joaquin as he poured him a glass of water. "Oh, by the way, my name is Pedro. My dad found you, and we brought you back to our house. You didn't look like you were going to make it, let me tell you. The dog found you first, though, and he started barking; my dad came to look at what he was barking at.

"He was cooking, and it was my favorite meal, by the way. *Arroz con pollo.* You need to try it. Ever since my mother got sick, she hasn't been able to cook. She has something wrong with her blood, they said. Too much sugars or something. I'm not sure. They had to cut off her foot last year, so now she sits and watches *novelas* all day, and Dad has to cook. He's getting better, but it's still not as good as my mother's. But don't tell him that, because my brother made that mistake once, and it didn't go too well for him.

"Here, drink this; you need to get water back into you. We tried giving you some, but you kept coughing and spitting it out. Once, my *abuela* passed out, and we had to give her water to try and wake her up, but she just coughed and coughed and slapped my grandpa because she thought he was trying to drown her. He would always say, 'Don't tempt me, *cabrona*!' Of course, he would never say that loud enough for her to hear..."

He kept on speaking. Joaquin tried to keep up with everything Pedro was saying, but he would start many conversations and trail off and start others. He just lay there and looked on as Pedro spoke; Joaquin never even saw Pedro stop to take a breath. Joaquin finally was able to sit up enough to try and get a drink of water, and Pedro, without stopping what he was saying, put the cup to his mouth so he could drink.

"I tell you, my *abuela* was something else. I always loved to see how she could kill snakes with her bare hands; it didn't even bother her at all. Even though she was tough, she also had a soft side. One of my *tias* had a baby, and it came out, you know, *tonto*"—he twirled his finger around his ear—"and she didn't want it, so she was going to give it up, but *mi abuela* said, 'NO!' She took care of him, and even though the doctors told her that he wouldn't live long, she wanted to love him for as long as she could. The entire time he was with her, she would tell him '*Mijo*, when I die, I will take you with me because no one will love you like I will.' She always said that, and it sounded like a nice thing at the time.

"Then, one year, *mi abuela* had a twin brother, and he passed away just before *día de San Valentín*. Man, let me tell you, it really hurt my *abuela* because they were close. Well, later that same year, she passed away out of nowhere, and she wasn't even sick. *Loco*, huh? Well, get this, she passed away on a Tuesday, and, not even a week later, my cousin, the one she was taking care of, passed away. He was almost eighteen years old, and the doctors said he wouldn't live past five years old."

Joaquin could see the goose bumps on Pedro's arms, and he shook with a chill. Joaquin took a big gulp of water and choked on it, but kept drinking; it was so refreshing. Joaquin felt as if he were a dried-up sponge, sitting in the hot sun, with cold water just having been poured on it.

"*Tranquilo,* not so fast, or you'll get sick."

That didn't stop Joaquin, and he didn't slow down. He was drinking as if it were the last time he'd ever have water.

"You're going to get sick, *amigo*…oops, too late."

Joaquin started coughing, and the water he'd drunk came back up. He vomited the water all over the floor, and Pedro already had towels ready to clean it up.

A voice from another room yelled for Pedro, and he turned and told Joaquin, "Get some rest, and I'll be back later."

As Pedro was leaving, Joaquin was able to get out, "*Gracias.*" It was painful, and his throat hurt to speak.

Pedro nodded and left the room.

The following day, Joaquin was feeling much more revived, and he was able to hold down the liquids he put into his body. He was given a bowl of *caldo de pollo* to try to eat, and he was able to finish most of it. It felt so good to finally eat because he hadn't had much to eat for almost two weeks. Then it hit him. "*Ay, Dios mío,* I've been gone from home for almost two weeks. Cati must be worried terribly about me."

Just then, Pedro walked in and asked, "Who is Cati? I heard you say that name many times while you were out. I figured it was your *novia* or *esposa*. I had a girlfriend not too long ago, and she was really pretty. We were doing great, and then, for no reason, she left. I don't know why; it was crazy. She didn't even say good-bye or leave a note. I mean, what kind of person leaves and does not tell someone good-bye, or at least leave a note? Well, I guess it was for the best. I don't think her father really liked me anyway. He would always say I was *molestándolo*. Whatever, she's long gone, and I have more time to help my family.

"I do a lot for my family here, and I know *Diosito* will bless me one day for all that I have sacrificed for them and all that I do. Do you believe in *Diosito*? A lot of people think it's nonsense, and they'll go on and on about how, if he's real, why does all this bad stuff happen, and how can he allow good people to die. It just gets annoying when they go on and on about how much they don't believe in him, and I'm just here wondering why it bothers them that I do believe. You know what I mean, *amigo*?"

"*Perdóname*, Pedro, but I think I need to use the toilet." Joaquin had interrupted Pedro because he didn't know how long Pedro would keep going if he tried to hold it. It was extremely difficult for him to try and stand because his muscles were very weak, and he still had cramps in his legs and lower back.

Pedro was quick to help him stand, and he put one of Joaquin's arm's over his shoulder and walked him over to the toilet. Pedro was shorter than Joaquin, but he was strong and stocky, so he just about carried Joaquin to the bathroom. Joaquin was able to walk himself once he reached the bathroom.

When he finished, Joaquin looked at himself in the mirror and hadn't realized how much his face was bruised, and he had cuts on his upper lip and over his left eye. After seeing his face, the pain began to follow, and he started feeling every bump and scrape he had on his body. He washed his face as best as he could and fixed his hair and combed it with his fingers. Upon exiting the bathroom, Pedro was there and offered assistance, but Joaquin declined and wanted to go on his own. "*Gracias*, but I think I can do it. My name is Joaquin, by the way. I can't thank you and your family enough for what you have done."

"*De nada, mi amigo*. We're just glad we were able to find you when we did. If it wasn't for Chucho, we probably never would've found you there by the fence. By the way, we have to fix that fence you broke. My papi wasn't happy that it was broken, and now he has to go into town and get more wood for that post, and the man that sells the wood always tries to start a fight with my father because my father looks like the man his wife left him for. He is a little bit *loco*, if you know what I mean. It never ends well, and then a lot of the time we don't get what we came for. He has a daughter that is pretty and…"

Joaquin was getting dizzy, standing there and listening to Pedro go on about the *novela* in the town, so he tried to go back to bed.

Pedro followed and continued on with his story. This time, Joaquin thought he heard him stop to breathe once.

"Can you believe that? She has three babies and doesn't know who the father is. Her family is ashamed to talk to her, and they ignore her when they see her in the town. So, do you have any children? I'm here with no wife, so I obviously don't have any."

Joaquin was starting to understand why Pedro's girl-friend left him, and he'd only known him for a couple of days. It was still nice to have someone to speak to or, in his case, someone to talk to him.

After a few days, Joaquin was back on his feet and able to get around without any problem, and he finally came to the dinner table with the rest of the family. The house smelled of fresh tortillas and *comino*. The salsa in the air was scratching Joaquin's throat and eyes, but it all smelled so good.

Pedro was excited to eat because his father had made his favorite *arroz con pollo*. His mother and father were already sitting and eating as Pedro served himself and Joaquin a plate. His father didn't waste time before asking what happened and why Joaquin was almost dead when they found him.

Joaquin wasn't sure if he should go into full detail on the events that had led him to their backyard, so he just simply told them that he was kidnapped by some men and was able to escape them, but was trapped in a village for a little while until he was freed. Then he came through the tunnel of water and ended up in the creek behind the jungle in their backyard.

As Joaquin was telling his story of how he got there, he noticed the tortillas were not round like his mother would make them, and most were burnt. He then took a forkful of food and almost stopped breathing. The chicken was very dry. The rice tasted as if it were added to the salt, and it was undercooked. Joaquin didn't want to be rude, so he just poured the salsa all over it in hopes it would help the taste.

Pedro's father said, "*Perdón, pero* I don't cook as well as my wife, but we need to eat, and this is Pedro's favorite dish."

Joaquin looked at Pedro, and he was practically face first on his plate and eating as he spoke, without taking a breath. He stopped a second to look at Joaquin and said, "This is the best!"

Pedro's father asked, "Are you sure you came from the creek? There isn't anywhere to come from through the creek. It comes from the mountains and the rock formations there in the jungle."

"See, I told you, Papi, that I remember seeing people go into that mountain through the creek when I was little," Pedro, taking another breather, said.

"Pedro believes that people live beyond those rocks, and he's seen them come in and out of there. No one has ever seen them, but he claims he has. Plus, the only people that ever lived in this area was our village, and hundreds of years ago there was some other village on the other side of the mountain, but they died off many years ago. No one has ever seen or heard from anyone from that side of the mountain."

Joaquin didn't want to tell him his story since it sounded too farfetched, and no one would believe him anyway since the natives were thought to have died off. So, he listened instead. He learned that Pedro was only two years younger than he, and he had actually started at the university, but quit after his mother became ill. She didn't talk at all. After they cut off her leg, she felt useless, fell into a deep depression, and stopped speaking. She would eat and watch her *novelas*, and that's all. During the day, Pedro would help care for his mother while his father worked, and then, in the evening, Pedro would go off to work at a steel mill. They had followed this routine for some time, and it seemed to be working. Pedro was still young, however, and he wanted more for himself.

The following day, Pedro and Joaquin hopped in the truck and headed into town. Joaquin was still a little cloudy from all the lying down he had done over the past few days, but decided he needed to get moving. On the way to the lumberyard, Pedro just kept on talking and telling all the juicy details of the townspeople. It started becoming amusing and not so annoying to Joaquin. He was actually enjoying it.

Once at the lumberyard, they retrieved the materials they needed for the fence and headed to the checkout. The owner was there, and when he saw Pedro, he immediately turned his smile into a scowl and walked off very upset. You could hear him saying as he stormed off, "That *hijo de puta* better not be here!" The two of them looked at each other and laughed. It felt so good to laugh, despite all that Joaquin had endured. The smile and laughter didn't last long, though, because it would always make him think of Cati, her smile, and how it made him feel. He needed to see her and make sure they were all okay.

"Hey, *amigo*, what's wrong? Where did you go?" Pedro asked him.

"*Ay, perdóname*, I was thinking about *mi novia*. I am really worried about her. I tried calling this morning, but there was no answer," Joaquin replied.

"Well then, let's finish this fence really quick, and then we can go see her. I'll drive you home, *amigo*, no problemo."

"No, I can't ask you to do that," Joaquin said apologetically.

"*Pues*, you're not asking. I'm telling you we can do that after we finish this fence. We need to leave now because the owner is coming back, and he doesn't look happy," Pedro said with urgency.

They both chuckled as they finished paying and ran off to the truck. In the side-view mirror, Joaquin could see the crazy old man holding up his fist, yelling at them, and chasing them a little ways as they sped off.

On the way back, Pedro asked what town he lived in, and when Joaquin told him, Pedro had a surprised look on his face. "Oh wow, that small town is many hours away. Good thing I don't have to work for the next two days. We can go, and I will leave you with your *amor*."

Joaquin was very thankful and told him he would somehow find a way to repay him. Pedro just brushed it off and said it was not necessary, that is what *amigos* did for each other. Plus, he didn't have to fix the fence by himself, so that was payment enough.

They reached the house, and they quickly got to work, finishing the fence in no time. After, they took a shower and readied for their departure. They ate some food they prepared, and Pedro called one of his *tias* to come watch after his mother while he was away.

The ride back to Joaquin's home with Pedro was long, but he was anxious and scared at the same time. He only thought of Cati and wanted to apologize to her for everything, to just hold her and see that smile once again. He had drowned out Pedro several times, because hearing him go on and on, about who knows what and who knows who, was a bit overwhelming. Either way, he was so grateful for the ride back and glad that Pedro was such a truly nice person. For whatever reason, Joaquin felt very comfortable around Pedro, and he told him everything that he had gone through to get there from Honduras. When he told Pedro about his mother, Joaquin could tell it actually hurt Pedro; he was, for the first time, at a loss for words.

"How are you not really *loco* yet?" Pedro asked jokingly after many moments of silence after Joaquin finished his story. "Wow, that is just crazy that you had to go through all that just to get to America."

Joaquin simply nodded his head in agreement.

They were almost to the farm when Joaquin decided not to drive up to the house, for fear of being seen and Cati's *tio* finding out about his return. He told Pedro to pull over about a couple of miles from there; he would just walk the rest of the way.

After he got out of the truck, the smell of burnt wood and ash was still heavy in the air. Joaquin remembered seeing the farm being set on fire when he was taken away. He began to jog towards the farmhouse, and he knew a way to go so he wouldn't be seen. Everything was so quiet, and it didn't appear anyone was working. He felt a cold chill run up his spine because the silence seemed unnatural. The more farmland he crossed, he started to realize that they burned more than a few crops. Everything had been burned.

He passed by the agave barn with the tequila, and it was burned to the ground. In front of it was what looked to be the remains of a horse and a man. This caused Joaquin to stop in his tracks and fear took hold; he didn't want to find the worst.

He slowly turned in the direction of the house and saw that it too was burned. It appeared to have happened pretty recently, though, because there was still smoke coming from the windows of the house. He thought to himself, *There is no way he would hurt his family like this. Why would someone do this to prove a point?*

The only building not completely burned was the closer farmhouse that was next to the main house. Joaquin ran to it and, inside, looked upon a sight that he didn't know was possible. Stuck in the ground, there were three pitchforks standing upright, and on those pitchforks were three severed heads of men who had worked for Señor Hernandez. It caused Joaquin to gag, but not throw up. He was able to hold it back, but the sight was horrendous. Flies had already swarmed the heads, and the smell of the decaying bodies indicated that it had been a few days already since they were killed. When Joaquin tried to walk past this gruesome scene, several rats ran from the bodies that were stacked near the impaled heads. That's when Joaquin became scared and started for the house.

He called out to Cati like a mad man, ran to the house, and checked everywhere he could. But Joaquin found no signs of life or anything indicating that Cati was in the house. He yelled out for her, more and more, with pain in his voice. When he went back outside, he saw Pedro standing in the yard and looking up at the side of the house, his hat off and over his chest. Joaquin, with tears already streaming from his eyes, slowly walked over to where Pedro was standing, trying not to look, but preparing himself for what he was about to see. When he looked up, he just fell to his knees and cried and screamed. There were three bodies hanging from a charred tree. The bodies were unrecognizable, but you could clearly tell it was two women and one man.

Joaquin, unable to control himself, started punching the ground and yelling, "I want to kill that *hijo de puta*! That fucker is dead if I find him!" Joaquin had never felt this type of rage and hate, because his mother had always taught him to be nice and respectful towards everyone. This had to be the exception because there was no way he was going to be nice and forgiving to a man who had killed two of the people in his life whom Joaquin loved so dearly. He had to die and nothing was going to stop Joaquin.

He cut down the three bodies, and Pedro helped him bury them, as well as the workers. The entire time, Joaquin was brewing up more hate; he wanted to go find El Warden so he could kill him. That man needed to die more than anyone in the world. As he was lowering the three bodies into the ground, Joaquin made them a promise that he would not stop until that man was killed for doing this to them.

It was a very quiet ride back to Pedro's home. Then Joaquin burst out, "I'm going to kill that *hijo de puta*! I don't care how long it takes or if it costs me my life. I will not stop until he's dead!"

Pedro was quiet for a moment; then he said to Joaquin, "Well, there may be a way for this to happen if you really want to get revenge and kill that *cabrón*."

This caused Joaquin to stop thinking of ways to kill El Warden and look at Pedro with interest.

"You know how I've been going to work in the evenings at the steel mill? Well, I haven't actually been going to work at the steel mill anymore. Sometime about a month ago, a man approached me when I was on break, and he told me about a secret police force that they were training so that they could go after bad men like that. These men were not a part of the police or the *federales*, so they knew they wouldn't be bought by the drug lords. They sought out people that were fed up with how they were being treated, kidnapped, and killed by these men. They even brought in a real Navy SEAL from America to show us how to fight and do things that most of the usual police here would never know. I'm telling you this because we are always looking for perfect recruits, and by the looks of it, you are definitely a perfect candidate for this. We can show you how to fight and to kill without being seen, and we can put a stop to all these men that are doing harm to our country."

That sparked something in Joaquin that he didn't think was possible after he just had to bury Cati, his love. He listened as Pedro told him the basics of what to expect and what he needed to do if he was truly interested. Before Pedro could even finish, he quickly grabbed Pedro by his shirt, at his chest, and said, "When and where do we start?"

Chapter 8

HDM

"Okay, guys, one last stop before we get to where we're going," the officer yelled out loud.

They stopped at some gas station to fuel up before that last stop. It felt as though they'd been driving for such a long time. Others questioned if they were still in Texas, while a few knew that this was a long bus ride. You could almost drive for an entire day and still be in Texas.

Some of the men were beginning to become restless and wanted to walk around. They would say they needed to use the bathroom just to stretch their legs. One officer was getting irritated by constantly having to unlock them from their seats to use the bathroom, but he knew he had to do it anyway; he just took his time. Another officer walked up and down the aisle, making sure that everyone was okay and that there were no issues. Many of the men had fallen asleep and were resting on each other or had their heads against the windows. Joaquin wasn't one to sleep much, especially on these types of rides. He had been on plenty of bus rides, and he knew enough not to fall asleep.

There was an officer towards the front of the bus, and he was very friendly. He was speaking with the men, asking them where they were from, assuring them that they would be fine, and telling them not to be worried about what was going to happen to them. That put many of the men at ease, but they all had so many questions; that officer did his best to answer.

They departed for their next stop. An officer had purchased some cases of water, and after leaving the gas station, he handed them out to whoever was thirsty. Joaquin looked over and noticed Wilbur had fallen asleep. *I guess that's what happens when you speak politics. You get too tired to stay awake*, he thought to himself and laughed.

"*¡Escuchen, chicos!* Listen up, guys. You were brought here to become one of the elite *a todo México*. We all here have lost family members or have been affected by a corrupt system that will not take responsibility for what they have done and have allowed. You have been hand chosen because we believe that you are individuals that are ready to make a difference and help liberate our country from the men that have been stealing, killing, and raping our families. They have their police and their *federales*, but we are stronger, faster, and smarter than all of them combined. You will be trained how to fight harder, move without being seen, and, most importantly, kill faster than anyone who comes across our paths."

This was the opening statement that Joaquin heard as he was in a room with ten other men.

"*Me llamo Capitán Alvarez*, and you will go through some of the worst training you have ever encountered. You men will be living and breathing killing machines and unstoppable by any police force here in Mexico. You don't have any family because they were either taken from you or killed by the men we hunt. You are no longer alone in this battle, and we will all give our lives to make sure you have revenge for your family that is no longer here. So, are you ready to give your life for the HDM (*Hijos de México*), put down your life for your brothers, and fight until your very last breath?"

That question brought out a loud "RAHH, RAHH, RAHH!" from the men standing in the room. Joaquin, yelling this chant, felt the strength and unity in the room, and the ten men sounded like one thousand as their yells bounced off the walls. The men were so eager and ready to fight for their country, and even die if need be. Tears of joy and sadness from losing their families, and now being able to do something about it, poured from the men's faces.

Clapping and shouting continued until Capitán Alvarez held up his hand and gave the men their final instructions. They were not to discuss this with anyone, for fear of being found out by the enemy.

Joaquin was fortunate to have been allowed in this group. Normally, they didn't allow new recruits to bring anyone in without an already established member seeking them out first, but once they heard Joaquin's story and who he was running from, they welcomed him.

"You have no idea how long we've been after that *pinche cabrón*! He always manages to slip away because he will sacrifice anyone to make sure he stays alive," Capitán Alvarez stated. "I just can't believe that I am standing in front of someone that was able to get that close to that *hijo de puta*."

Capitán Alvarez was about as tall as Joaquin, but much more built than he. He had been in the American military and was a Navy SEAL. He was originally from Mexico, but his parents moved him and his family over to America, and he was able to get an education and learn about fighting and killing. He came back to Mexico when he learned that men had hijacked his parents' vehicle one year as they were visiting family for the holidays. That really upset Capitán Alvarez; he was enraged when he went to the police, asked what they knew, and they blew him off, telling him that they were "working on it." That's when he decided that he would learn as much as he could, come back, and take revenge on all those who were involved. He started building his army, and they had been tracking down as many of those men as they could, but he knew he needed a bigger army. It was taking longer to find those who were worthy since there was so much corruption in Mexico. So many people were poor. They would accept money to keep quiet and give up anyone who opposed the corrupt officers; otherwise, they themselves would be killed.

"I don't mean to question you or anything, Pedro, but how did you get chosen to be in this? I mean, you have both of your parents," Joaquin asked.

"Well, *amigo*, when I was little, maybe about seven or so, my parents were killed by some men trying to kidnap me. These men were looking for young boys to work in their factories and help with jobs that only small people can do, and not worry about being paid. They shot my mother and even shot my papi, but he was so tough that it didn't kill him. He managed to kill the two men with his bare hands before dying from his wounds. I was sent to stay with my parents now because their son was kidnapped, and they've never heard from him. Some friends of my dead parents knew what happened and hid me, for fear that they'd return and try and take me. That's when they found my new parents, and I've been here ever since. They've been nothing but good to me, and I would give my life for them and my country."

Joaquin was taken with emotion as he spoke with many of the other men that evening, and the majority all had similar stories. It just seemed crazy that, despite all that these men had gone through, they were still willing to give up more. They each had reasons to give up their lives. Joaquin knew his own reason, and nothing was going to change his mind.

On their way home, Pedro was excited for Joaquin to start as soon as possible. Joaquin was eager and ready to start then and there, but Capitán Alvarez told them to be patient. They would be contacted when they could begin.

"*Muchas gracias por todo*, Pedro. I can't thank you enough for all that you have done and, now, for giving me this opportunity to help in such a way. I don't know how I can repay you," Joaquin began telling Pedro. "My main goal was to get to America, start a new life with Cati, and have a family of my own. That *hijo de puta* took that away from me and her, and now he is going to pay."

"No need to repay me, *amigo*," Pedro told Joaquin. "Just be the man I think you are and help us bring those bad men to justice for our families and our country. I mean, what else do you have to do?" They both chuckled, and, the rest of the ride home, Joaquin just thought about Cati.

A few weeks passed, and Joaquin was walking around town just wasting time, with nothing really to do. He was looking at how everyone was very friendly with one another and the vendors would help each other. He was greeted with smiles everywhere he went. It just seemed as though everything were perfect in this little town. Children playing with their makeshift scooters in the roads and others throwing a ball back and forth to one another. It was just a typical day. That was when Joaquin noticed a speeding, dark SUV pull up to a storefront.

Several men jumped out and entered with guns raised and pointed at the people inside. After the men ran inside, screaming and yelling started as people ran frantically from the store. Gunshots echoed throughout the village, and many onlookers began to gather to see what was going on. The men exited the store with three teenage-looking girls, and anyone who tried to stop them was shot and killed without any remorse.

Seeing this enraged Joaquin, and he ran in that direction to try to save them somehow. He wasn't entirely sure how, but he just knew he needed to do something, rather than just sit there. Just as he was getting ready to approach the SUV, a van drove up in front of Joaquin. Two men with their faces covered jumped out, put a bag over his head, and dragged him into the van. He started trying to fight his way free and managed to punch one of them in the face and kick him in the knee, causing the leg to buckle. The one man holding him from behind put him in a choke hold that caused Joaquin to go unconscious. Just before the lights went out Joaquin could smell lavender and vanilla on the man choking him.

The smell of ammonia flooding Joaquin's nose immediately woke him up. He began to cough and was slightly dizzy from being choked unconscious. He realized he was tied to a chair and was still blindfolded. Someone had used smelling salts to wake him up and, just to torment him, had left it there a little while longer than needed. That was followed by a punch to the face.

"Who do you work for?" he heard a low, calm voice ask.

Joaquin initially thought it was El Warden and his men who'd caught him. Although, it didn't sound like El Warden, so he was puzzled by the question. If it had been El Warden, he wouldn't be wasting his time questioning Joaquin like this; he'd be in a ditch. Another punch to the face and then his stomach, which made him hunch over, and it pushed all the air out of his lungs. He coughed several times, trying to catch his breath.

"Who do you work for?" the calm voice asked again. "If I have to ask again, you will not like what happens next. So it would be best if you just answer all the questions easily without stalling."

Joaquin was confused because he didn't work for anyone, and he had no idea what this person wanted. "I don't work for anyone—"

Joaquin was stopped by an electric current going through his body. He bit down on his teeth; his jaw hurt from how hard he was clenching his jaw. For a moment, his hearing got muffled, and his vision darkened. The shocking stopped, and the pain lingered a moment, but it was a relief when the current was turned down. Joaquin screamed in agony as he hadn't felt that type of pain before. Joaquin received another punch to the face.

This time, the voice was louder and more stern, "I can do this as long as you want. If you don't answer my questions, I have more electricity to give. Your choice. Now tell me! We know you are working with a group that is going after men that they think are hurting this country. We want to know who this group is and who is in charge. Just answer those questions, and we'll set you free." Someone came very close to Joaquin's face when the man was speaking, and Joaquin could smell the same lavender and vanilla. So, he knew this was the same man who had kidnapped him.

This really upset Joaquin because, whoever this was, they knew he had been approached by the HDM; they wanted information on HDM, and they were willing to do whatever it took to get it. Still feeling that man very close to him, Joaquin spit in his face and said, "¡Vete a la mierda! I am not telling you anything because I have nothing to tell."

He was then shocked again, but stronger and longer this time. Joaquin's head was shaking and his teeth rattling. His entire body felt as if it were on fire, and he began sweating; he urinated on himself. This went on for about thirty minutes—the questioning and then the shocking or punching. When they realized he could no longer hold his own head up or even speak, they stopped.

Two men removed him from the chair and dragged his half-lifeless body to a dark room. It was cold and the walls and floor were cement. The smell of mildew filled the room; there was no light but from the cracks on the door they'd come through. The heavy door was made of steel, and it had a small tray slot at the bottom.

"Get used to this, you'll be here for a while until you decide to speak to us." Another voice spoke as they closed the door.

When Joaquin came to a day later, he was in pain from being shocked so many times. He couldn't feel his legs; they felt as if they were asleep. He did feel cold from lying on the hard floor. His eyes adjusted to the little light from under the door, and he could see that the room was smaller than a jail cell. He noticed two bowls near the door, and one was flipped over. When he was able to move closer, he could see that the bowl that was upright had some type of slop in it. It barely had anything in it, and it was mainly liquid. When he tried to smell it, it smelled strongly of vomit and cumin. He just let the bowl fall, and its contents spilled onto the floor. There was no way of telling what time it was and how long he had been there. He felt around the room, and it was completely empty, besides those two bowls and himself. The walls were damp with moisture, and the mold and mildew made them slippery. The cement was draining the warmth from Joaquin's body, and he tried to curl himself up in a corner and stay warm, but the cold wall on his back only made him shiver even more.

What is going, and why am I here, was all he continued to think. He tried to replay what happened leading up to his being captured, but nothing was triggering any notion as to why he would've been taken. He knew that these men were not the same men who were shooting at that store. Those men didn't wear masks, and they had an SUV that was well kept. They had on nicer clothes, and most wore blazers. In comparison, the van that he was taken in was old and white. Also, the men all wore masks, and their clothes seemed more like uniforms. He thought maybe they were just helping those men keep an eye on their backs while the men in the store did what they were doing. Then he considered it might be El Warden, but, knowing how much El Warden wanted him dead, Joaquin ruled that out again.

So, who has me, and why are they trying to get information from me, he questioned over and over. He didn't have any information for them, and even if he did, he knew well enough not to give them any. He knew from experience that, the moment you give up any information, you are killed and the information you gave is used to kill more people.

There was a pounding on the door, and the little tray flap opened up. This broke Joaquin's train of thought for a moment. He tried to get to the tray slot to see who it was, but he was still too slow, and his muscles hadn't fully woken up. The person on the other side of the door opened the tray flap, slid another bowl under it, and quickly closed the slot. Joaquin tried to yell out, but the tray slot slammed shut, and the brief bit of light in the room was gone again. He made his way to the new bowl, and it contained the same slop as the other bowl.

Out of anger and frustration, Joaquin threw the bowl against the wall and yelled, "¿QUÉ QUIERES DE MÍ?" He continued to yell, "¡Qué quieres, qué quieres!" over and over, while banging on the door, in hopes it would get some reaction from whoever had him captive. When he didn't receive the reaction he was hoping for, he just sat back down and curled up in the corner to find some warmth.

The following day, he was awakened by the door's opening. Two masked men in all black entered the room, put another hood over his head, and dragged him out of the room. Joaquin was fighting a little, but he knew he was too weak to even escape from these men's grasp. Along the path that they were walking, Joaquin could hear other men yelling in pain while being yelled at and asked them the same questions they had been asking him. When they stopped walking, he heard some chains being dragged on the floor, and then his hands were handcuffed. He heard a machine overhead making some noise, and they grabbed his hands and hooked some chain around his handcuffed hands. They tightened the cuffs until almost cutting off circulation to his hands. He heard the machine again, and this time he felt it lift his hands. It continued to lift his hands until they were well over his head, and it didn't stop. He felt the pull on his wrists as the chain tightened and he was lifted off the floor. The cuffs were cutting into his skin from his weight pulling down on the chain. His feet were barely off the floor when it stopped.

He'd hung there for what seemed like forever when he heard a voice, which startled him, say, "Sooo, are you ready to talk?" The raspiness of the voice was deep yet loud. "You're not strong enough to hold out, so you should make it easy on yourself and just speak."

Joaquin tried to be vocal, but his throat and mouth was so dry he couldn't speak.

"Oh, I'm sorry; did you try to speak? I can't hear you with this on your head," the man said as he was pulling the hood off Joaquin's head. "I know you think that, if you speak and tell me what I want to hear, I will just kill you. So you feel that if you hold off from saying anything, it will stop the inevitable. I can assure you that 'I' will not kill you if you speak to me. Just tell us what we need to hear, and you will be spared." He paused for a moment, waiting to see if Joaquin would speak, and then noticed how dry Joaquin's lips were. "Well, it appears that our hospitality isn't what it should be to gain your confidence. Allow me to get you something to drink. You appear a little parched."

Joaquin heard the machine above him start again, and this time it lowered him. When he was on the ground, the chains were removed from his cuffs, and he was carried over to a table and strapped to it. One strap on his forehead, another across his shoulders, one over his hips, and another over his knees. Separate straps for his wrists and feet. He looked on as the masked men brought over a giant jug of some liquid, and, before they started pouring it on Joaquin, they covered his face with a towel. They began to pour, and the water started filling up his nostrils, and it caused his mouth to open from an automatic reflex. The water then filled his mouth, and it caused Joaquin to cough and cough. He was trying to catch his breath, but every move filled his nose and mouth with water. Ten seconds later (which felt like eternity), the towel was taken from his face, and the water stopped. Joaquin gasped for air and coughed the water out that he had breathed into his lungs.

"Okay, let's try this again now that I've been gracious enough to give you a little bit of water. Who do you work for, and who is in charge?" The question came again, followed by a hard blow to his stomach.

Joaquin coughed again in pain as the little air he had left exited his body. He gritted his teeth and clenched his fist very tightly, trying not to let these men break him.

The man asking the questions gave the signal, and the towel was placed back on Joaquin's face, and the water started up again. This time, as they held the towel over his face, someone grabbed his neck and squeezed. Joaquin was finding it difficult to stay conscious, and he shook back and forth, hoping they would stop. Twenty seconds this time.

"We can keep going, or you can make this stop. Your choice, *cabrón*. Tell us what we need to hear, and you will be free. That simple, otherwise, we can keep going until you think you're a *pescado*."

When they removed the towel from his face this time, Joaquin was enraged. He coughed a few times and then just sat there staring at the men with hate. He locked eyes with the man asking the questions.

"So, do you have something to say, or shall we continue?" the man said with a smile on his face.

Joaquin took a second before he spoke. He thought of his mother and how she was tortured and killed, of what his friend at the missionary had done for him, and then of what Cati had to go through before being found hung and burned. "I don't know what information you're looking for. I can't tell you what you want to know, but what I can say is, if I did have that information, I wouldn't tell you a fucking thing just to stay alive. I've seen people like you and what you do to others. Whoever you're hiding from and trying to get information on, you must be scared of them, and I hope they find you. Go ahead and just kill me because I will not tell you a damn thing. *¡Vete a la mierda!*"

The man demanding the answers slowly walked over to Joaquin, knelt down so that he was next to his ear, and said, "Welcome to the *Hijos de México*, Joaquin. You passed day one of training."

With that, he was released, and the men all took off their masks. Joaquin was still so enraged that, when he was released, he swung at the first man he could reach, but that man quickly moved out of the way. He grabbed ahold of Joaquin, hugged him, and patted him on the back. This was followed by the other men doing the same, hugging him and patting his back to congratulate him for passing the test. Joaquin was still confused as to what just happened, but realized they weren't trying to hurt him. He started looking around and saw all the men in the room as they were smiling and high-fiving each other. They then led him to another room where he was to be briefed on what to expect next.

Upon entering that room, Joaquin saw that there were only three other men there. They all looked like Joaquin—unbathed, bloody faces, and covered in their own urine or feces. Their faces appeared familiar, and Joaquin realized that they were the men from the other night when they were introduced to Capitán Alvarez. When they saw each other, they each had the same puzzled and confused look. They went to one another and asked what happened; they all had the same story.

It took a while before Capitán Alvarez arrived in the room, but he was very happy and was giving the men praises for a job well done. Throughout that conversation, Joaquin noticed that no other men had come into the room; there were just the four of them. He wondered if they had changed their minds about joining, or if they hadn't passed the test. If they hadn't passed the test, then what happened to them? So many different questions began flooding his mind, and he could see some of those same questions were filling the minds of the other men.

When Capitán Alvarez finished speaking, the men were invited to sit and enjoy some food as he knew they'd be thirsty and hungry. They all attacked it like mad men and ate until they were almost sick. After the feast, they were shown where the showers were and given fresh clothing to wear. That shower felt so good when Joaquin stepped in. The water was nice and hot, and he just stood there letting the it hit him. It was almost as if he were washing off a different version of himself, and he was ready to become someone new. Once he was dressed, they met in a large warehouse that had different sections to it, but it was all open, and you could see what was going on in each section.

The men stood there admiring each other's transformation, and Joaquin kept looking at the quality of the clothes and boots they were given. The belt they were given only had a single pouch with a knife in it. Upon inspecting the knife, he found that the blade on the knife was dull and almost felt fake. Joaquin figured this must be part of the training, so he just put it back in the pouch and waited for further instructions.

Joaquin was standing around with the other men when he saw Pedro running in his direction. When he reached him, Pedro gave him a huge hug and pulled him tight. "Good job, *hermano*! I'm so proud of you. You did it. Welcome to the *fraternidad* and day one of training."

"This is day one? I'd hate to wonder what lies ahead if, after all that, this is day one," Joaquin said, sounding a little irritated.

Pedro laughed and said, "*Tranquilo, hermano*, that was just to see if you're really ready. It'll all get better from here on out. I went through it, and everyone here that is with us has gone through it. *¡Hombre!* I almost wanted to quit, but I didn't want to disappoint my family if they ever found out I was here, so I just pushed forward. I know it will be hard to believe, but I didn't say a word the whole time I was here. Imagine if I did speak; they would probably run me off for talking too much nonsense, or get tired of me talking and talking without really giving them any information. I was told that you were the strongest and didn't budge when they were shocking you. I cried a lot when they hit me with the shocks. Man, I pissed and shit at the same time, I think. So, how did you like the water over the face? That is something new they started. Way worse for most people. That's usually when people are ready speak. Not you though; you were tough, *hermano*. Let's go get a drink."

Joaquin missed half of what Pedro was saying because he was wondering about the other six men who weren't there. "So what happens if you don't pass? What do they end up doing to you?" Joaquin asked.

"As far as I know, they are let go and told to go home and to never speak of this again," Pedro answered. "We are all too excited to get to training, so we don't worry about those that didn't pass."

"Okay, *caballeros*, listen up. You have the rest of the day to play grab ass; it's time to get to work, and we have a shit ton of things to go over," Capitán Alvarez said to the four men.

He took them on a tour of the training facility, and Joaquin quickly turned his attention to everything that was going on and what he was going to be going through. The question of what happened to the other men still remained there, but he figured he'd ask at a later point in time. For the present, he was going to concentrate on learning as much as he could so that he could go after El Warden and give him the justice he deserved for all those he had taken from Joaquin.

Chapter 9

Bait and Switch

"This is the last stop before we get to your temporary home, *caballeros*," one of the officers walking up the aisle stated.

Joaquin noticed that they were in San Antonio earlier as they passed the giant cowboy boots. Anyone passing through can't miss them unless they're trying to. The traffic was a little heavy, especially since it was rush hour, so they weren't going very fast. They pulled up to a building near some busy roads, and they waited for the officer controlling the gate to finish with a vehicle in front of them. He was a younger officer who seemed eager to be there and not someplace else. The officer quickly finished checking the vehicle in front of their bus and then waved them forward. He began doing his checks and asked the driving officer for the paperwork. Once he was satisfied that everything checked out, he opened the gate and waved them through. After they passed the gate, they pulled into an area designated for the buses.

"*Bueno, señores,* when you hear your name, please stand up." They called out half of the names for the men in the red uniforms. These men had court appearances the following day. They stood up when they heard their names. Another officer unlocked the shackles being held to the floor so that the men could step out of them and make their way off the bus. The others on the bus, out of curiosity, continued to look at those men as they slowly made their way into the building. Joaquin could tell by the looks on their faces that they were just amazed at most of the new things they were seeing in America, despite it being from a bus and being shackled. Most of those men had never been outside their villages, so seeing the tall buildings and magnificent structures was amazing to them.

Wilbur was almost leaning over on top of Joaquin, trying to look outside the window. He was so struck by everything and how colorful and big many of the buildings were. "Oh wow, if only *mi esposa* could see this. This is so *magnífico.* One day I hope to bring her here so she could see how this all looks."

Joaquin knew the likelihood of that actually happening was very low. Most just worked to send money to their families because it was cheaper to send the money back than to bring the family to the United States. The cost alone to bring them over was really expensive, so they just left them in their hometowns and sent what money they could.

Joaquin often thought of the family he wished he had and wondered where he would've raised that family. There were some beautiful places in Mexico, and life was much simpler there. But America had so many opportunities, and he actually liked snow and the way it looked falling. He pictured himself with Cati and his children, playing in the snow, making a snowman, and having snowball fights. Seeing their cheeks red from the cold and icicles forming on their hats and earmuffs. Then going back into the warm house to try to get the wet clothes off and sitting by the fire while Cati made that hot chocolate with the old lady on it. He knew that was impossible now because Cati was gone, and he was on this bus heading back to the jungle.

The taste of his own blood had become all too familiar over the years, and it still carried that same coppery taste. Joaquin had been in training for the past eight months. Between combat training and English classes, he didn't know which was harder. He did, however, advance to being top of his group. With their completion ceremony coming up, he must be able to beat Capitán Alvarez, along with a few other officers, one at a time with only a sixty-second break between.

The first couple of officers were easy to defeat, and as he continued, Joaquin's strength was dwindling and he was becoming fatigued, but he still had more to go. Each time he received a new opponent, they were stronger and more skilled than the last. The first course started on a mat; it consisted of wrestling skills and being able to subdue your opponent if you were ever on the ground. Then they had moved on to hand-to-hand combat, in which they used their hands and feet to either knock out your opponent or make them quit. Next, they had to, with the use of the blunt knives, try and kill their opponent with the least amount of cuts possible and without getting cut yourself. The knives they used were a special type that released markings on the blade end to mimic being cut. The fourth course was accurately being able to shoot someone from one to two miles away, followed by a close-quarters shooting course. There you'd have to walk through different scenarios, shooting the bad guy and saving as many villagers as you could. Some were real people posing as the bad guys and the villagers, and others were the paper targets. The difficult part is that, while you're trying to complete that course, the officer you're up against is looking for you and has a rubber-bullet gun ready to shoot you. You have to be able to get through that course undetected and kill the men holding the villagers hostage.

If you were able to complete all those courses, you had to take on three officers at once in hand-to-hand combat. If you by chance were able to make it past the three officers, you were left with your final course, and that meant taking on Capitán Alvarez in an all-out, free-for-all hand-to-hand combat, but this time with a real knife. You had to not get cut and either cause your opponent to yield or have your knife to his neck or kill spot. No one had ever come close to defeating Capitán Alvarez, and today he was going to make sure that Joaquin didn't either.

Joaquin was mentally ready to take on Capitán Alvarez and knew he needed to be at the top of his game. It just would have been much easier if he weren't so worn out and already beat-up. With his nose already bleeding and a cut over his eye, Joaquin walked around for a bit, sizing up Capitán Alvarez and waiting to see what his move would be. Most people taking on Capitán Alvarez tried to quickly muscle their way and go at him full force. That gave Capitán Alvarez the opportunity to see what they were doing and to react before they could get the best of him. Joaquin didn't do this, so it threw Capitán Alvarez off a bit.

Joaquin continued circling around, and they both just stared at each other, waiting for the other to strike first. They didn't have the knives in their hands; instead, they were both lying on the floor, between the two opponents. So, as they did a dance around each other, they would look at the knives and then back at each other. Joaquin would fake as if he were going to grab a knife, and it caused Capitán Alvarez to move towards him or jump back.

"Whenever you're ready, *cabrón*. I don't have time to be here all day. I have things to do and your mother to fuck!"

This upset Joaquin, and he charged at Capitán Alvarez, who quickly kicked Joaquin in the chest and made him fall backwards. Joaquin was already tired and in pain, so it really took a lot of energy out of him. He was slow to get up, but was not ready to stop. Joaquin decided that he would act as though he were going for the knife and then try and spear Capitán's legs to bring him to the ground.

"Oh no, no, *mijo*, I know what you're thinking, and that won't work either. You're too slow, and you're just not good enough. Why do you think Cati died? You were a coward, and you didn't even try to save her."

Joaquin became so enraged he just wanted to hurt Capitán in such a way that he would be able to experience an ounce of the pain Joaquin felt throughout each day, knowing that his mother and Cati were dead and he couldn't do anything to stop it. Joaquin dove for the knife, but was met with a foot to his face. This opened up more cuts on the bridge of his nose and his upper lip. He couldn't concentrate because he was dizzy, and for a second, the lights went out, but he was able to snap out of it. Despite the anger he had towards Capitán Alvarez for using his family to get into his head, he knew he needed to bury it. Otherwise, it would cause him to make wrong decisions, and he wouldn't be able to concentrate on what he was doing.

Joaquin forced those feelings out of his mind, but instead thought of El Warden and was able to channel that hatred into what he was doing. Capitán Alvarez came in for another kick that was aimed for Joaquin's side since he was on all fours, trying to stand up. Joaquin saw this and grabbed Capitán Alvarez's foot, stood up while holding it, and threw him to the ground. Capitán fell where the knives were, and he quickly stood up with a knife in his hand.

"Good, *pendejo*, put away all your feelings, and now you may have a chance," he told Joaquin.

Joaquin tried to grab the knife on the ground, but Capitán Alvarez sliced his arm before he could reach it. Joaquin jumped back, examined the cut on his arm, and realized it was not that deep.

"Nope, it's not going to be that easy. Come on, let's go, reach for it again," Capitán Alvarez continued to taunt Joaquin in order to get into his head and throw him off so he would make bad decisions.

Joaquin finally had enough and tried to end the cat-and-mouse game. He faked diving for the knife, but planted his hands on the ground in order to do a forward flip. Capitán Alvarez didn't see that coming, and when he went to cut Joaquin again for reaching for the knife, he didn't see Joaquin in motion for the flip. Joaquin managed to get his feet over his body fast enough that he landed on Capitán Alvarez's back, causing him to fall face first onto the ground. Joaquin then drove his elbow into the back of his head, picked up a knife, pulled Capitán Alvarez's hair back, exposing his neck, put the knife there, and told him to surrender.

What Joaquin didn't realize was that Capitán Alvarez was able to put his knife against Joaquin's side, and when Joaquin told him to surrender, Capitán pushed his knife harder into Joaquin's side, making Joaquin pull away and realize he may not have defeated Capitán after all. Joaquin stood up, off Capitán Alvarez, and he threw his knife down in anger.

"If you have your opponent in this position, you do not have to take the time to be theatrical and pull their head back to cut their throats. Save that for the movies. You only need to take that blade and drive it into the back of their skull or straight down into their spine. We're not here to win an Oscar for the most dramatic way to kill someone. Better luck next time, Joaquin."

Joaquin walked away feeling defeated, even though he was able to get that blade to Capitán's neck.

Pedro came running after him and was very excited. "*Santa Maria*, Joaquin, that was crazy! No one has ever been able to do that to Capitán Alvarez. Damn, that was an awesome move you did. I didn't even get past the three officers. I was too worn out, but, wow, you were awesome."

The emotions from thinking about his mother and Cati flooded back, and Joaquin didn't feel like celebrating. He simply walked back to the shower room to clean up and rest. On his way back to his bunk, he was grabbed by a few other men. They put a sheet around him and dragged him out of the building. Joaquin, tired and exhausted, had no idea what was going on, but tried to fight off the men who had grabbed him. He was able to get one punch in before they dragged him away.

Once outside, four masked men held Joaquin down, and another stood over him with a hot branding rod. The symbol on it was that of an *H* with a circle around it. The right side of the *H* was longer on top, and it was a cross. As he pressed it to Joaquin's chest, he stated, "Welcome to *los Hijos de México, cabrón*. You are one of us now. Anywhere you go, if you ever need anything and you see this symbol, they will help you."

The smell of burnt skin filled Joaquin's nostrils as that hot iron was held to his skin. Hearing the sizzle of his skin and seeing the smoke rising would've been too much for most people, but the pain was bearable, compared to what Joaquin had endured in his lifetime.

Several months after the completion ceremony, Joaquin had been moved up a couple of ranks for his performance in the course. Since he had nowhere else to be, he stayed there at the training facility. He was ready to train every day and learned more and more as time went on. Pedro still went home so he could care for his mother and pretended that he was working. Those who could stay at the facility did, and the others went home and showed up every day when they could. They only required that you show up every day, put in 110 percent effort, and, most importantly, never speak of this to anyone.

Joaquin had grown accustomed to the lifestyle there at the facility, and, even though he had not been taken out on a mission yet, he just figured he probably wasn't ready. He continued to train and perfect his skills. He could get in and out of a room without being noticed, which helped when he no longer wanted to be around people. Learning from those elite killers had turned him into someone he almost didn't recognize anymore. His muscles had filled out, and he was now one of the biggest in the group. He'd grown a full beard, and the scars on his face told a story that could fill most people's lifetime.

There was one thing that told him the old Joaquin was still there. When he slept, he still dreamt of his mother, Sister Ana, and now Cati.

One evening, he dreamt he was walking through the farm on a sunny spring morning. No clouds in the sky and butterflies gliding on the light breeze. He felt calm and at peace for the first time in a long time. No troubles or worries within his dream. It felt so real, and he didn't want to come out of it; that's how peaceful it was. There was happiness walking through the farm and seeing the agave grow. He would chop a few and prep the agave for making the tequila. Not even a drop of sweat was made; that's how perfect everything was.

He heard his mother call out to him, "Joaquin! Supper is ready!"

"Yes, hurry and clean up!" Cati's voice followed.

He just loved hearing their voices and knowing that they would be at the house, preparing dinner and all laughing and getting along, with Sister Ana blessing the food and always giving everyone the best advice. Then, as he began to walk to the house, it got farther away. The more he moved closer, the farther away the house seemed to get.

Then, Cati came out to see about Joaquin and called to him, "There you are, what are you doing? Come on, let's go; we all want to eat."

Joaquin waved out of fear and yelled back at her, but she didn't see him in that form. She only saw him walking towards the house. He was invisible to her. Then he noticed she wasn't looking at him when she called out. He saw a man walk up to the house, grab Cati by the waist, and pick her up. She laughed, put her arms around him, and kissed him. Joaquin became enraged because he wasn't the man with Cati. He tried to get to her, but he couldn't reach her. The house just kept moving when he tried to get close to it.

His mother poked her head out the door and told Cati and the man, "Okay, you two lovebirds, let's go. Otherwise, you'll have to go to Confession first."

They all laughed, and as they went inside, the man slowly turned, and the only thing Joaquin saw was a wicked grin on his face and the mangled right side of his face, with his eye red as fire. Claws grew on his fingers as he put his hand on Cati's waist as she walked in. He looked straight at Joaquin, knowing he couldn't reach them, and then slowly turned back and proceeded into the house.

Joaquin couldn't believe what was happening; he was trying to wake up, but he felt trapped. Trapped in his dream from waking up and trapped because he couldn't reach Cati and his family. Then he heard screams of terror, and as quickly as the screams were heard, they stopped. Joaquin was still trying to get to the house, and when the screaming stopped, it was as if he was released, and he was able to run to the house.

The sunny day turned to overcast, and the house seemed old and gloomy. There was no noise at all. He could see the trees swaying and birds flying, but not a sound was coming from anything. There was only a single sound he could hear, but he didn't know what it was or where it was coming from. He ran inside the house, hoping to find them inside, but it was empty. He ran through the house, calling out to anyone, but again there was no one to be heard, and the only sound he could hear he couldn't make out. No matter what part of the house he was in, the noise was the same, as if it came from everywhere. When he couldn't find anyone in the house, he decided to run outside. Once outside, the sound went from a single sound to a few, each sounding as if they were from different times, but all the same sound.

"What is that sound?" he kept asking himself. Then he realized what it was. It sounded as if a rope was being pulled really tight. Outside his dream, he was drenched in sweat, and he was still trying to wake himself up. Inside, he kept looking for where that sound was coming from.

Then, at last, he finally came to the sound. He looked up in the tree next to the house, and he saw the three of them hanging from the tree. Their faces were destroyed beyond recognition, and their bodies were burned. Below the swinging bodies, that man with the fiery eye held three hearts in his hand and smiled as Joaquin stood in shock at what he was seeing. The man bit all three hearts at once and threw the hearts at Joaquin.

Just before they hit him in the face, Joaquin woke up yelling. He couldn't catch his breath as he was panting so hard. That had to be the worst dream for him yet. When he woke up, Pedro was sitting there, just looking at him as if he had been there for some time, just watching.

"¿Sabes qué, hermano? You really need to go see a curandero for that dream you're having. It seems like they're getting worse, because when we found you, you didn't yell that much. Te ves muy feo cuando duermes. You don't have a good sleeping face." Pedro made an ugly face with his mouth wide open and let drool fall out the side.

That made Joaquin a little upset, and he threw his pillow at Pedro, but then he started to laugh, and they both broke out in laughter. Joaquin could always count on Pedro to lighten the mood and to crack a joke when needed. Most of his life was nothing to joke about, or even share laughs about, but Pedro was able to do that in many situations, which helped Joaquin cope with everything.

Joaquin told Pedro, "No more *curanderos* for me. I've seen more than I ever want to, and I have no intention of seeing anything more."

The next morning, their wait was over. Capitán Alvarez called a meeting, separated the men into groups, and told them that they were being given their first mission.

"All right, ladies, this is what you've been waiting and training for. Tonight, we have located a small group of drug runners planning on making a move, and we will be there to make sure that doesn't happen. *La policía* doesn't know about this, and neither do the *federales*. This is a quick in-and-out mission to get your feet wet and so you can see your skills put to work for real. Don't fuck this up, and we'll be able to find who they were working for and continue up the chain."

The men started becoming excited and began cheering amongst themselves.

"We have a small window, and we don't have time to waste. So get your shit, and let's go make someone's night really bad."

The men ran off to the locker rooms; they were handed gear as they entered. Joaquin looked at all the high-tech gear they received and was astonished.

He was with Pedro when he asked, "So, do you know where the money comes from to supply us with all this great equipment? I mean, even this facility is crazy. I'm just curious who funds it since they obviously aren't police or *federales*."

Pedro just shrugged his shoulders as he was getting dressed. "Well, *mejor* it's from the Pope himself. He's the only one that I can think of that has more money than the government."

They looked at each other and just gave a sarcastic stare as if to say that was highly unlikely. Along with all the high-tech items they were given, Joaquin decided to keep his father's knife with him, just in case, and also as a good-luck charm.

In the van, they were given further instructions as to what they were to do and when to strike. They were told that they would position themselves similar to fire ants. When they were all in position, they would wait, and a signal would be given. That's when they were to strike all at once. Quickly and quietly in unison. They should make minimal noise and not draw attention. Once they took out their targets, they were to leave immediately and meet back at the designated area for departure.

"I will remind you that if you are seen or captured, the HDM will not claim you, nor will they come back for you. These missions require your ability to get in and get out undetected and are strictly voluntary. Each one of you is essentially acting alone and will be treated as such if you get caught. Simply put, don't get caught, and you get to go home."

Joaquin looked over at Pedro; his eyes were closed, and he was moving his lips. Pedro's faith in God had always been strong, so Joaquin knew he was praying. Joaquin was very nervous, and he could feel a knot in his stomach from the anxiety building. As he looked around, many of the other men in the van were saying a prayer as well. He decided he may as well say a prayer, in hopes that God would help and protect him in what he was going to do. As he finished his prayer, it was almost at the same time as the others, and they all made the sign of the cross as they kissed the pendants around their necks.

They pulled off to the side of the road about two miles from where the drug traffickers were. They would go on foot from there so the traffickers couldn't see them coming. As they jumped out of the vehicles, each man was focused and determined to help be a part of something greater than himself. Most importantly, they were all dedicated to exacting revenge on these men for taking their families from them.

It was complete silence for those two miles, and the only thing you heard was the men's breathing and footsteps as they ran through the trees to get set up for their attack. It was very humid that evening. Joaquin was expecting his clothes to be sticking to him, but the quality of the garments prevented that. In fact, the clothes actually made him feel cooler as he ran. He already was enjoying the perks of working with this organization.

Pedro was only a few paces behind him. When Joaquin turned to look, he saw a different person than the man who was always talking and cracking jokes. Pedro appeared to be made for this and seemed to know this was where he belonged. Joaquin felt the same and knew with his brothers he would be okay.

As they approached the area that was the meeting place for the drug exchange, they were running single file, but then they broke off into different groups to set themselves in attack position. Joaquin could see vehicles with men standing outside them, carrying guns, and looking around. He thought to himself, *Well, now it's time to see if all this training really works.* Before he got into his position, Joaquin said another quick prayer, and then told Cati and his mother that he loved them and that this was for them.

All the men positioned themselves quickly and quietly without being spotted. There were ten men in total on Joaquin's team, and it appeared to be about thirty or so men at the drug deal. So, they needed to take out at least three men each, making the least amount of noise possible. They'd practiced this before, and they'd been able to make it sound as if only a few shots had been fired, even with all of them shooting at once. They just needed to time it perfectly when the signal was given.

Joaquin was in his position and had his sights on the first man he was taking out. That man was close, and then another man about a few meters from him would be the next, followed by his partner in the vehicle. Joaquin was planning the entire scenario in his head; he knew what he was going to do. He calmed his breathing, and he could hear his heart racing and pounding through his chest. Sweat was running down his face, but the masks they were wearing stopped it from getting into his eyes. Patiently waiting for the signal seemed like an eternity.

There was a group of men standing in the middle of all the parked cars, and they were speaking. Then, some briefcases were about to be exchanged when a shot fired off, and the two men engaged in the exchange took the same bullet through their heads. That blood splatter hit the few men around them, and it caused them to duck down. That was the signal they had been waiting for.

With a gun in his left hand and a knife in his right, Joaquin quickly jumped from his cover, looked at his mark, and fired at his head; the bullet found its place right in that man's ear. As that man fell, Joaquin, still in motion, front-rolled, aimed and shot at the man a few meters away, and ran to him before he could fall. He then used him as a shield to get closer to the vehicle and rammed his knife into the last man's eye, twisted the blade so there was no mistake he was dead. He moved without thinking; he had trained his body to think for him, and it was showing with the precision and speed all the men were taken out. Joaquin noticed one other man in the back seat of that vehicle and quickly acted; he was able to shoot him before the man could get his gun out to fire back.

Joaquin looked for Pedro to be sure he was okay, and he saw him removing his knife from a very large man's neck. From the looks of the wounds, it took many times to put him down. He grinned at Joaquin, and they did a quick scan to be sure they had gotten everyone.

As quickly as they reacted, it was all over. Without saying a word, the ten men picked up any brass from their guns and ran back through the woods, headed back to their rendezvous point. Not a single cheer or word was said on the ride back to the facility. The men had a look of shock at what just happened, and their eyes had gone from nervous and scared to fierce and content. They all felt that they were able to avenge their family members just a little with taking out those drug traffickers.

Back at the facility, as the men walked through the doors, the cheers and celebrating began. They had executed and completed their first mission with speed and precision. The men were giving each other high fives and hugging when Capitán Alvarez spoke.

"*Bueno, caballeros*, you did a fantastic job tonight, and that is how we should always conduct ourselves in the field. Those *hijo de putas* had no idea what hit them! This was your first mission and a great start; there will be many more to come after this. Celebrate for now and feel proud that you have contributed to liberating Mexico from those cocksuckers that think they can steal our country."

This was followed by more cheering and several loud rounds of "RAH, RAH, RAH!!" The adrenaline kept the men up for several hours that evening, and when they finally lay down, Joaquin and Pedro were in their bunks, but they both were still very much awake.

"Man, what a night, huh, *hermano*?" Pedro asked Joaquin. "Those *pendejos* didn't know what hit them. The way you did that front roll was awesome." Joaquin shrugged his shoulders as if not trying to gloat. "Even though they probably weren't the ones that killed my family, it still felt very good to stop those men from possibly hurting other families," Pedro added.

Joaquin didn't talk much about what happened that evening. He was amazed at himself for being able to kill those men so easily. He never thought himself to be a killer before, nor did he want to hurt people for fun. He simply wanted to stop these men from hurting more families and from destroying this country. People were becoming so afraid of these men that they would not say anything negative about them for fear of it reaching the traffickers, who would come after them or anyone in their families. Joaquin had grown to love the people in Mexico because they were very nice and eager to help others in need. It just made it difficult for people to help when traffickers were telling them, "Either you do as we say, or you die." So many people wanted change, but couldn't get involved out of fear of what might happen to them or their families. If it were only the traffickers that were the problem, many more people would be able to resist because they would be able to rely on the police and the *federales* for help. Unfortunately for the citizens of Mexico, the system was too corrupt for the people to depend on, so they just kept to themselves and did nothing. That was why the HDM was building its army—so it could show the great people of Mexico that they were not alone.

Pedro kept talking about everything from that evening, and then he trailed off on other things as well. Joaquin began feeling himself fall asleep as he started coming down from the adrenaline rush.

Over the next two years, many more missions took place similar to their first one. As word spread about the HDM, they were noticing more and more men being used at the exchanges. At one point, the ten of them had to take on sixty or so men. This no longer was a quick and quiet execution. It required the use of more bullets and a few of them getting injured. Thankfully, everyone on the team had been able to escape death so far, but a few had taken a bullet or two. Due to their speed, precise killing strategies, and quickly leaving the scene, they started becoming known as *Los Fantasmas*. The ghosts.

For Joaquin and Pedro, the most they had received in terms of injuries were cuts from a knife, bruising from punches, and a few jammed fingers from trying to gouge out eyes. Each time they went out, their skills increased, and they'd been able to kill their enemies with ease.

One evening just before another mission, Joaquin was thinking about his mother and Cati. He started questioning if what he was doing was the best way to honor them or to gain revenge for them. Either way, he didn't feel as though they were getting any closer to liberating Mexico than when they first started. Despite the way he was feeling, it did not change the way he performed his elite killing tactics. The most he needed was two bullets to kill anyone, and he always enjoyed the smell of the gun smoke when they finished. Using his hands and a knife was, in his mind, very easy, and it came as second nature to him.

He didn't even have to think about what do anymore; his muscle memory did all the work for him.

It had been another quick in-and-out mission at a small, hidden airstrip. On their way back to the rendezvous point, Joaquin realized that his father's knife was missing. "Oh shit, I need to go back!" Joaquin said.

Pedro was behind him when he said, "What? What do you mean you need to go back? You know the rules. Once we finish, we can't stay there; we must get out fast."

"I know, but you don't understand. I dropped my father's knife, and I have to get it back." Joaquin had stopped running at this point, and Pedro stopped as well. "I promise I'll hurry back. Plus, at the pace we're running, I can easily catch back up. Don't worry."

"You better, *cabrón*, because I'm not going to get stuck scrubbing floors again. That was my last toothbrush I used because of you," Pedro said before taking off.

Running as quickly as he could, back to where he believed he'd lost his father's knife, Joaquin had to stop and take cover before arriving at the spot. He was crouching near some barrels because, approaching the area, he noticed moving vans similar to those his unit was driving. Thankfully, there was a dead body hunched over a barrel, which gave Joaquin better coverage. He sat quietly, trying to see what was going on.

When the vans arrived and stopped, several men from the HDM jumped out and broke off into teams. One team gathered all the weapons that were useful from the dead men on the ground, as the other team took the money and the drugs. All he heard was, "*Rapido, rapido*, we need to hurry; the plane will be here shortly."

Joaquin was a little confused about what was going on; then he saw Capitán Alvarez exit one of the vehicles, and he wasn't happy. "What do you mean this shipment was short? It was supposed to be twenty-five kilos and a couple hundred pounds of *mota*."

"*Sí*, Capitán, but they only had half here. I'm guessing our intel was bad," one of the other men told him.

"Well, that is not acceptable; *el jefe* is not going to be pleased. He was expecting that full shipment. Those *hijo de putas* think that they're going to get away with only giving us half, they're sadly mistaken. Get that fucker on the phone now!"

Another man dialed a phone and handed it to Capitán Alvarez.

"Hey, you cocksucker! You told me it was a full shipment, and we only have half. I don't care what you have to do, but by the time we get there, you better have the other half; otherwise, *sabes lo que pasará*." He threw the phone, said, "Let's go," and twirled his hand over his head.

Joaquin was so distracted by Capitán Alvarez that he didn't realize that the team picking up guns was almost on him. When he looked back at those guys, he hit the barrel with his knee. He froze where he was and held his breath. The noise caused that team to look in his direction. Thankfully, it was dark, and they couldn't see very well. They drew their guns and pointed them in that direction, and they slowly made their way to where Joaquin was.

Joaquin had to think fast and find an escape route. The way he'd come was not an option as those men had that path covered. They were getting closer, and Joaquin's options were getting fewer and fewer. He was getting nervous, and his heart was pounding loudly. As the men closed in, one of them came around the side to flank him, but when they got there, it was only the dead body on the barrel.

Joaquin was able to get through the taller grass and head towards the shack that was nearby. They didn't seem like they were interested in that, so he figured he could escape from there. He climbed through a window that was in the back of the shack, and, once inside, he realized it was more than just a shack. From the outside, it appeared to be a very small shack, but on the inside he quickly learned it was big enough to hold a plane. It wasn't a small plane either; it was a Kodiak, and when Joaquin looked through the window, he saw it had the other half of that shipment Capitán Alvarez was looking for.

Joaquin thought to himself for a second, *Why are they taking the money and drugs from these traffickers, and why is Capitán Alvarez so hell-bent on getting the other half of the shipment?* Nothing was making sense at the moment, and he was hoping this wasn't something worse than what it looked like.

The men outside cleared out, and Joaquin was about to make a run for it to make it back to the rendezvous point, but a plane and other vehicles were approaching. There was no way for him to get out of there without being spotted. There were several vehicles, and the plane kicked up a bunch of dirt as it made its way down that small runway. He saw a couple of men walking towards the shack. There was nowhere to hide, so he looked inside the plane. There was a cargo space at the bottom of the plane, and Joaquin was hoping it was empty. It was; he crawled inside and covered himself with a tarp. The shack doors were opened, and one man got inside the plane, while the other was starting preflight checks. The man outside hooked the plane to a tug and started pulling it outside.

Joaquin heard the man inside the plane on the phone, and he didn't sound Mexican. "Yeah, it was a massacre. No one was left alive. They even took their guns, those greedy fucks. No, no, they didn't find the other half. Fuck them, they're just some small cartel thinking they can steal all of our shit and sell it off as theirs. We do all the fucking work, and these assholes come and steal it. They're on borrowed time. We'll find them and feed those cockroaches to their dogs. Yeah, I'll be there in a few hours."

When he hung up, the engine started, and Joaquin could no longer hear what was going on. Joaquin was dumbfounded at what he just heard. Was he really working for a drug cartel? That would explain why they had an endless supply of funds to get them the best equipment. Then, the more Joaquin thought about it, it made sense. They bring in someone with Capitán Alvarez's skills to train men, and they are unstoppable. They go in and kill the competition. Because the unit is told to quickly fall back to the rendezvous point, they clear out, not knowing the other team is taking the drugs and money. Then, Joaquin figured they all had been chosen because it was easy to influence them; use the loss of their family members as a way to motivate them to kill anyone who was deemed a trafficker or a threat to other families.

The thoughts sickened Joaquin because, all this time he thought he was fighting for the good of the people, he was actually one of those men he vowed to kill. Waves of emotions were flooding Joaquin because, if he had known what this actually was, he never would've joined. He had lost his mother and the love of his life and was no closer to getting to America since he had spent so much time learning to kill people. It enraged Joaquin that he could be so gullible and naïve. He'd seen the signs, and even questioned it several times, but not enough to actually get the answer he just discovered tonight.

Joaquin finally felt the plane start to land. He had no idea what he was going to do and asked himself, *Why the hell did I get into this plane?* He thought of several scenarios, but all led to him getting caught and dying one way or the other.

On the ground, Joaquin was getting ready to accept his fate yet again. He waited for them to open the door and find him. The engine died, and he heard several men outside the plane. Then they began unloading the plane. Joaquin decided, if he had any chance of getting out of this, he would need to move as far back in the cargo hatch as possible. Once he repositioned himself, someone opened the cargo door and looked inside. Joaquin held his breath and didn't move at all. The man looking inside was satisfied that nothing was in there and closed the door.

A short while later, he heard a voice say, "Okay, we're finished; let's go. Put the plane back where it belongs, and the first drinks are on me."

Joaquin realized that the men had all been speaking English. He waited about an hour after the plane was put up before he attempted to get out. He wiggled his way out of that cargo space, and for a man his size, it was no easy task. He looked around and saw that it was daytime already, so being able to use the dark was out of the question. He peeked through the windows of the hangar and noticed other buildings around. This was a much bigger airstrip. Joaquin kept looking to get the lay of the area; then he saw it. He almost fell back in disbelief.

"*¡Qué carajo!* Is that an American flag?"

Chapter 10

Cutting Off the Heads of the Snake

After leaving the last building, an officer said it would be a short one-hour drive south to the facility they would be going to. Joaquin was scheduled to be deported along with a hundred or so other Hondurans, but needed to wait a few days. It seemed like a long process to them because they couldn't just send them back. They had to go through the process and wait for enough people to fill a flight to send back. Many of the men there didn't want to stay for such a long time, but from Joaquin's experience, that paperwork shit took forever, and so they must wait.

That frustrated the men because, the whole time they were in these holding facilities, they weren't making money. If they weren't making money, then they couldn't send some back to their families. Also, many of them shared an apartment with other guys trying to support their families;

with one gone, they each had to pick up that one person's share. That took money away from them and their families.

There were some people whose visas had expired, and with no money to fly back home, they just stayed past the expiration date, turned themselves in, and waited for the process to be sent back home. Joaquin saw that as a genius idea. People often question, if the process takes so long and you're losing money, why go through that in the first place? Shouldn't you just stay home with your family? Over the years, from what Joaquin had seen, it was worth it for most because back home they had absolutely nothing and they couldn't feed their families. This way, at least they took a chance, and, if successful, they knew they could provide for their loved ones.

Joaquin remembered hearing an old man once say, "If you sit and do nothing, nothing will ever happen. If you get up and do something, something will always happen." Joaquin believed that was why most people took a chance at coming over—because if they sat and did nothing, then they, along with their children, would die.

Joaquin always saw it as easy for someone with all the opportunities to look down on those who had none. Even though that irritated him beyond measure, he still didn't allow that to change who he was and always tried to better himself any way he could. Not to please those who looked down on him, but to please himself so that, at the end of the day, he wasn't sitting and doing nothing.

Wilbur was talking with a few of the other men on the bus, and then he turned to Joaquin. "*Señor*, will you try and come back when they send you home? We were talking about that, and I really don't have much choice since I have to feed my family. The others are pretty much in the same boat. It's hard being away from our families, but we have to do what we can for them. Am I right?"

Joaquin nodded his head in agreement with him. Getting to America was not their main goal, but to provide for their families and make sure they were okay had always been good reasons for them to make the trip.

Joaquin was pacing back and forth in the hangar. His mind was racing, and there was no plan for what he was to do next. He had spent all his life trying to get to America, but something always got in his way and stalled him. Now that he was actually here and, this time, he hadn't even been trying, he had no idea what to do. With all that he just learned about the HDM and who they really were, Joaquin was glad to be away from them. But Pedro was still fighting for them, and if Joaquin hadn't known who they really were, then Pedro surely didn't know either. If he went back, they would question him on where he was and why he didn't follow commands. Joaquin was not ready to revisit the type of interrogation they did.

He knew one thing for sure; he couldn't stay in the hangar and think about it. He needed to keep moving and make a plan. First thing first, he had to get out of the HDM uniform. Anyone seeing him in those clothes would question why he's dressed like that; the uniform would definitely draw unwanted attention. Joaquin looked around and was able to find some work clothes in the hangar, but they were a little too small. They had to do for now because there wasn't time to go shopping. As Joaquin was getting ready to leave the hangar, looking out the window for his escape route, that's when he felt a hard object pressed to the back of his head.

"Okay, partner, I don't know who you are, and I'm going to need you to turn around before I pull this trigger. No one should be here, and I will not hesitate to pull this trigger." The voice was really calm, but the slight cracking in it led Joaquin to believe the man speaking was also very nervous.

Joaquin knew he didn't want to hurt the man, so without using lethal force, he did a maneuver and was able to take the gun from the man and place him in a choke hold with his own gun to his head.

This freaked the man out, and he shouted, "Whooa! Wait. Hang on a sec. Don't kill me!"

Joaquin asked, "Who are you, and are you working with those men that brought this plane?"

"I just manage this hangar. I don't know those men. They pay me to keep people out of here, and that's all. I swear!"

Joaquin could feel the man trembling in his grasp, so he knew he was telling the truth. He let him go, but still held the gun on him.

The man stepped back and held his hands up. "Look, I don't see those guys ever. They call me when they leave, and then I show up to check on their plane. If you ask me, I think they're government workers because I showed up early one time, and they had jumped into government-issued vehicles."

This confused Joaquin, and he didn't know what to think. He thought to himself, *If these are government men and the people that I was helping aren't who they proclaimed to be, then I have been helping and killing for the men that I wanted to stop in the first place. If they are being helped by the government, then I need to get as far away as possible.* This cut Joaquin emotionally pretty deep because he was using the death of his mother and Cati as fuel to get rid of these types of people in order to liberate Mexico. He now felt as though he'd betrayed the people of Mexico and those he loved.

With this newfound knowledge, Joaquin wasn't sure what to do next. He knew he needed to get away, but what about all those men who were fighting under the wrong pretense? They needed to be told. How could he notify them without being killed in the process? Joaquin's mind was racing a million miles an hour.

"How far is the border from here?" Joaquin asked the hangar manager. "I need to get back to Mexico right away."

"Oh, you can't get there on foot; we're just south of Tucson, Arizona. That's about sixty miles to the border," the man answered.

Joaquin had never heard of this place and wasn't sure where he was exactly. The man saw the puzzled look on his face and pointed to the map on the wall close-by. The man slowly moved towards it and showed Joaquin where they were and how far the border was. As he was looking at the map, Joaquin sensed another body in the room and heard something behind him. The person behind him swung a large pipe at him, but Joaquin was already in motion to move out of the way. This caused the man managing the hangar to go after the gun in Joaquin's hand. Joaquin just allowed his body to take over, and while the one man was grabbing his hand, he saw the man with the pipe come after him again. Joaquin quickly kicked him in his kneecap, bending his leg backwards; the man with the pipe fell to the floor and grabbed his leg.

Joaquin then headbutted the man holding his hands and trying to free him from the gun. When that man tripped back away from him, Joaquin raised the gun, pointed it at him, and pulled the trigger. Much to his surprise, the gun didn't go off, so he pulled the slide back and pulled the trigger again. The gun just clicked and clicked. This surprised the man as well because he had put his hands up in fear, thinking he was going to be shot.

When Joaquin realized that the gun didn't work, he reached for his own weapon, but remembered that he had to take it off in order to fit in the cargo door. The man then dove towards Joaquin trying to get his hands around his neck. Joaquin was much too skilled for this man and was able to move around him and use his own body weight to toss him over the other man who was still holding his knee and yelling in pain. Joaquin walked past the two men, picked up that large pipe from the ground, swung, and hit the hangar manager as he was trying to get back up. He fell to the ground with a loud thud and lay there groaning.

Joaquin thought about killing these men, but then realized that he was no longer in Mexico, so he could not do this without big consequences. He dropped the pipe and looked for the closest exit out of there. When Joaquin was about to exit, he noticed a vehicle pulling up, so he quickly slipped through that door and out of sight. He waited a moment, to see what that vehicle was, and saw two men exit the vehicle and go inside the hangar. After a few minutes—from what Joaquin could guess, the men who just arrived were questioning the men he'd left in the hangar—he heard two single shots. They weren't very loud, so he figured they must have had silencers on their guns. They casually walked out and looked around for a moment, maybe hoping to see whom they were looking for or to be sure they didn't cause any disturbance that would alarm anyone. Joaquin looked around, searching for his escape route, and when he turned back towards the men, he saw them take off in their vehicle.

I need to get as far away from here as possible, Joaquin kept thinking to himself. He noticed some people exiting the airstrip through a certain gate and decided to just blend in and attempt to leave through there. He figured, if he just followed a crowd, he wouldn't be noticed. He could figure out his next move from there.

Joaquin made his way to that gate opening and casually walked out. He noticed exit signs, and he was thankful that most of the people were still walking the same way as he. He did get a few looks due to his clothes not fitting him, but he just kept a straight face and didn't stop walking. Walking past a couple of security guards without issue made him feel a little more comfortable, until he passed by one guard who recognized the work uniform and the name on it, and knew that it didn't belong to Joaquin.

The guard called out to Joaquin, "Hey you, wait, stop, come back here!" The guard started walking towards him, but Joaquin acted as if he hadn't heard him, and he just picked up his pace. The guard quickened his pace as well and continued to call out to Joaquin, but he did not turn around for any of his directions.

Once Joaquin turned a corner that was out of the guard's sight, he bolted and started running. He immediately stopped and walked casually when he saw a couple more guards. Seeing a restroom close-by, Joaquin turned into it. In the restroom, he noticed someone in the stall; they had a bag on the floor and their coat hanging on the door. He quickly grabbed the two and headed out, putting on the coat as he left. The bag was a backpack, so Joaquin put it on and walked casually towards the exit. He noticed the guard by the doors looking and watching everyone going out; Joaquin didn't make any eye contact as he pushed the door open and left the building. He kept walking and just wanted to get away, as far as possible, before he could stop and gather his thoughts.

After about a couple of miles of walking, Joaquin turned and didn't see anyone coming after him, so he stopped a minute to figure out where he was. He looked in the bag and noticed it had some clothes in it; they seemed to be big enough for him to wear. Quickly changing his shirt, he put the backpack back on and continued walking. He had no idea where he was, but figured he'd just keep walking until he could find someplace where he would be able to figure out what to do next.

As he was walking, Joaquin was just struck by all the bright colors and how busy everything was. Cars driving back and forth, up and down the streets, and the people looked very similar to him. He always thought that, being in America, you'd only see a bunch of *gente blanca*. During his walk, he came across a gentleman who appeared to be able to speak Spanish, so Joaquin asked him if he could tell him where he was and how to get to a bus station.

The man answered in English and told him, "Buddy, I don't speak Spanish. I'm a native here."

Joaquin apologized, spoke in English, and asked again. This time, the man was able to tell him where he was and how far the bus station was. Joaquin thanked the man and started in the direction he was told.

He stopped a moment to inspect the bag further and found a wallet with about two hundred dollars in cash and a bottle of pills. When he opened the pills, he looked at them to see what they were; they read "LEMMON 714." He didn't recognize them, so he just tossed them aside. The bag also had keys and some papers, along with a bottle of water. Joaquin continued on to the bus station and was still cautious, hoping he was not found by those men in the car or the guards at the airport.

At the bus station, Joaquin was able to find a bus that would take him to a border city called Nogales. The attendant at the counter was very helpful to the customers ahead of him, and he noticed she had a slight accent. She wore small framed glasses on her face, and her makeup was neatly done. She chewed gum, and he noticed that the gum would pop every other time she bit down on it. The more Joaquin paid attention to the sound, the louder it became. He was taken by her smile. He hadn't seen a smile like hers in such a long time.

This made him think of Cati, and he became lost in his thoughts of her. He was no longer paying attention to the line moving and was only thinking of Cati's beautiful smile that he missed so much. He saw her calling out to him, "Joaquin, Joaquin…"

He felt a push from behind and heard the attendant calling, "Sir, please come forward."

Joaquin snapped out of his daydream and realized she was speaking to him. As he approached the counter, the attendant asked him where he was headed, and Joaquin told her to Nogales. She heard the accent in his voice, and her smile grew larger.

She asked, "*No eres de México.* You're from Honduras. *¿Verdad?*"

It surprised Joaquin that she was able to recognize that he was from Honduras just from speaking to him. He looked around to be sure that no one was coming after him from any direction.

"*Tranquilo, señor,* it's okay. I only ask because I'm from there as well, and I can tell you are."

Joaquin smiled and just kept quiet but alert, in case there was someone waiting around the corner for him. He waited patiently as she typed up the ticket for the bus.

She handed it to him, and when Joaquin tried to pay, she shook her head and pushed his hand with the money back. "It's okay; no need to pay this trip," she said, smiling again.

Joaquin took the ticket. *"Muchas gracias,"* he stated as he walked away and made his way to the bus. He had about twenty minutes before the bus left so he tried to find a place to sit and wait.

All this time, since before leaving on the plane, he hadn't thought of food or realized how hungry he was. His stomach started to rumble and make loud noises. There was a small stand that sold sandwiches and soda. Joaquin had never had an American sandwich until he was with the HDM. They had introduced him to many American foods since many of the instructors were from America. He found he really enjoyed sandwiches because there were so many different ways to make them. The typical quick food for him usually consisted of rice and beans, and maybe a taco of some sort, but they always had the same ingredients. When he discovered sandwiches, he felt a sense of liberation from the same taco routine. He found that he enjoyed a Reuben sandwich the best. Unfortunately, they didn't have that kind at this small deli, so he just decided to try the tuna salad sandwich. It was different from the other sandwiches he had eaten, but he didn't care since he was so hungry. He was just about finished eating when they called for boarding the bus.

Joaquin headed towards the area where the buses were parked, and as he passed that one attendant, she smiled and waved at him. Joaquin gave a smile back, but did not wave. He quickly glanced around and stood in line to board the bus.

Many of the people on the bus were either from Mexico or natives of Arizona. There weren't that many people on this bus as it was heading south. Only the buses heading north were very full. Joaquin was able to find a seat all to himself, and he dropped into it after first looking around to be sure no one was following him. After about fifteen minutes of waiting, the loading of the bus was complete.

The bus driver, a large heavyset American man with white hair and glasses, struggled to climb the steps. When he reached the top, clearly out of breath, he held on to a pole and reached into his pocket to pull out a handkerchief. He yelled out to the people on the bus to listen up as he wiped the sweat from his forehead after the struggle of climbing the stairs. He went over a few instructions and his expectations for the duration of the traveling. "Most importantly, no one is allowed past this line when the bus is moving." He pointed at a yellow line at his feet.

Joaquin was partially paying attention, but some commotion outside the bus caught his eye. He noticed several police cars pull up to the station; officers jumped out and headed towards the waiting area. Joaquin hoped that wasn't for him and was getting ready to jump off the bus and run if needed. As the officers disappeared into the station, Joaquin looked over at the bus driver; he was finishing speaking and getting ready to take his seat. Looking back and forth from the driver to the commotion outside, Joaquin started to worry. He didn't want to hurt anyone, being here in America, but the anxiety was climbing as the driver slowly turned in his seat and then took off his glasses to clean them. Joaquin looked over towards the station, and the officers were all looking around for someone; he knew they were searching for him.

The bus finally started, and Joaquin's stomach dropped when the officers started looking outside, where the buses were parked. Then, they went back inside the station. The bus couldn't take off fast enough for Joaquin. He let out a big sigh of relief as the bus finally left the station, and he could see the officers still searching the other buses. Joaquin turned back in his seat and thanked God for getting him out of there. The ride was not very long, given that it was only sixty miles, so Joaquin, relieved that he got away, closed his eyes for a moment. He had been awake for far too long and his body was feeling it.

Joaquin felt a tap on his shoulder, which startled him, and his body went into fight mode. He grabbed, by the shirt collar, the man who tapped him, and he had his knife out and to the man's neck before the man could even react. When Joaquin realized that there were several officers surrounding him with their guns already pointing, ¡Mierda! he thought, as he slowly put his hands up and dropped the knife. The closest officer then grabbed Joaquin and turned him around to place handcuffs on him. Now, being in America and given his current situation, Joaquin was wishing he were in Mexico. It was so close, but he didn't want to find out if he could take on this many armed

American officers just trying to escape back to the place he was running from in the first place.

He was escorted to a building there at the border gate and placed in a room that was very quiet. It had a single table in the middle and two chairs across from each other. On the table, there were a glass of water and a manila folder, along with a tape recorder. It smelled of mildew from the cement walls and old carpet on the floor. He noticed the large mirror on one side of the wall, which he figured to be a two-way mirror. The light wasn't very bright, but would occasionally flicker.

Joaquin was left in the room alone for some time. He didn't sit, only paced the room looking for his way of escape and waiting for what was to come. He had been tortured too many times to not expect it, and he was ready for what-ever they threw at him. He kept telling himself that he had to stay calm and be alert. Maybe they didn't know who he was, and maybe they'd just deport him, just as he wanted, so he could get back to Mexico and warn Pedro about what he was into. Then reality set in, and Joaquin thought that maybe they did know who he was and, they were holding him for the HDM, who, when they got there, would kill him for uncovering what they really were. Either way, he decided to stay quiet and see if there was even a slight possibility of getting out of this.

A man walked in holding another folder and a cup of coffee in his hand. He was tall and slender, with greasy hair slicked back. The cigarette hanging from his lip barely held on as his thick mustache with long handle bars pushed it every time he spoke. He told Joaquin to take a seat as he himself began to sit down. "Well, I was hoping to speak to Mr. Telemantes, but you aren't Mr. Telemantes, are you?" the man sarcastically asked. When Joaquin didn't answer the question, he continued, "You see, the bag you so kindly relieved Mr. Telemantes of was being tracked by my men. He was leading us to a warehouse that had stolen goods. Stolen goods that were being smuggled into the US and then sold off to the highest bidder. Now, you have to forgive me for asking, but WHO the fuck are you?"

Joaquin was a little confused at first, but then realized that he was not the man they were after. Knowing that, he hoped he could find a way out of this after all. He slowly sat down and thought about what he was just told and what he should say next. He decided to tell the man what happened.

"I'm terribly sorry, señor. I came to this country illegally, and I was hungry. I didn't have any money, and I needed to find a bus ride here so I could meet with my tio who had a job for me. I knew many people would be at the airport, so I decided to take someone's bag in hopes they had money in it. I'm really sorry, señor. I really didn't know what else to do."

"Well, I'd say you are one dumb son of a bitch, because you went and grabbed the wrong bag," the officer said while trying to hold back a laugh. "Where you from, Pancho?" the officer asked.

Joaquin told him he was from a little town in Mexico, but what he didn't say was that it was a town over from the HDM facility.

"Fuck, you are either dumber than you look, or just plain stupid, I tell you what. When you get here to the US, you don't hang around the border. You try and get as far north as possible." The officer gathered the items from the table and walked towards the door. As he opens the door to leave, he says, "Damn, boy, you really fucked up my operation here. I have been following this guy for weeks. Now I gotta fucking start all over."

The officer closed the door to the interrogation room and enters the room where another officer is watching through the two-way mirror. "Now what?" he asked the officer as he walked in.

"Fuck if I know. I'm just pissed that now I gotta start from scratch to get my guy that I was following in the first place. Then, I got Pancho over here fucking shit up for me. Fuck, just send him with the next shipment of wetbacks leaving in an hour. He's no good to me if he ain't Telemantes." That officer walks out of the room upset and slams the door.

Joaquin was sitting there wondering what was going to happen next. He had no idea if they believed his story or what was happening. After about forty-five minutes, another officer opened the door and called for Joaquin to follow him.

Joaquin stood up and slowly followed the officer. Looking around as he walked down the hallway with officers not paying any attention, he was thinking of the many ways he could escape from here, and they wouldn't even notice.

"Let's go, or you'll miss your ride to Mexico, Jose," the officer tells him.

Joaquin realized they bought his story, and he was now getting sent to Mexico without question. He felt relieved and concerned at the same time. Relieved because he didn't have to stay there, and he would be set free. But also concerned at how easy it was to tell them any story, and they bought it.

They stopped by an in-processing desk where an officer took his picture and fingerprints. He was then asked for his name, date of birth, and where he was born. All of which he lied about. He did not want anyone who knew his name to find out where he had been and where they dropped him off.

Once that had all been completed, he was escorted to the holding cell with other men who were also being sent back to Mexico. It wasn't long after that they were put in a fifteen-passenger van and taken to the other side of the border, just at the Mexico gate. As the detainees were getting out of the van, their restraints were removed, and they were told to head back to Mexico. A few pleaded with the officer to allow them back into America because they had nothing there, but the officer just pointed south and told them to go. As they walked back through the border gate, Joaquin saw a few men take off running together, heading towards the border again. He assumed they would try again later this evening to get past security.

Joaquin needed to get farther south, and he knew he wouldn't make it on foot for too long, so he just stayed along the main road, hoping to find a ride. Joaquin thought about calling Pedro at his parents' home, but didn't think that would be wise considering that would put Pedro's family in danger. He didn't know if anyone would be listening in on the phone call, so he didn't want to chance it.

A truck, which had hay and a few other men in the back, stopped, and the driver asked Joaquin if he needed a ride. He picked him up and took him as far as he could go. Joaquin continued finding rides until he was close enough to walk the rest of the way.

It was already nighttime when Joaquin arrived at the headquarters of the HDM. He did a quick perimeter check to see how many people were actually there that night. Then he walked behind a building where the men slept. He figured he would be able to get Pedro's attention and then tell him what was going on. As he slowly made his way, he heard someone talking, so he took cover by some trees so he could hear and see them at the same time. One of the men was an HDM member, and the other was dressed as if he was going out dancing, with really fancy boots, a giant belt buckle, and a large cowboy hat. The HDM member didn't look familiar, and the fancy guy seemed to be angry.

"We told you, *hijo de puta*, if you want to see your family alive, you have to give us more information on their next mission. El Warden is not a patient man and will kill anyone and everyone you know and love."

"Look, I told you to never come here when I'm here. I can only tell you what they tell me. They don't tell us when the missions are until an hour before it actually happens. I will have my tracker on when we go, and you can find me then. Until then, don't ever come back here again."

The fancy guy turned and walked away into the woods, and the HDM member, before walking back inside the building, looked around to be sure no one was there.

Joaquin couldn't believe what he just heard. El Warden had someone inside the HDM, feeding them information so that they could ambush them and take over. There was no way Joaquin was going to let Pedro walk into a trap. He needed to notify Pedro immediately so that he wouldn't get killed. He thought maybe he would be able to see Pedro there at the facility, but realized that this wasn't the place he should try and talk to Pedro alone. Joaquin decided to wait for him at his parents' home and maybe speak to his family so that they could discuss the danger they were all in.

Joaquin wasn't sure how much Pedro's family knew, so he just waited for Pedro outside. He did a quick walk around the house and made sure no one was around watching. It was turning daylight already, and Joaquin knew Pedro would be coming home shortly. After about thirty minutes past the time he usually got home, Joaquin started to get concerned as to what was taking him so long. He was getting a little anxious and decided he would go to the facility and find him. Even rescue him, if needed. When he started to leave, Pedro was walking up the road, but behind him in a car were a couple of men who stayed a distance from him, but weren't trying to hide either. Before approaching the house, Joaquin had left a note in the mailbox in hopes that Pedro still checked it before going inside.

When Pedro opened the mailbox, he saw the note, but didn't grab it. He was able to read what it said without picking it up: "Meet me where you and your father found me." He simply grabbed the other two letters that were in there, held one of them up to the light and opened the other, just to show the men watching they were only mail. He then walked into the house. The car that followed found a spot just across from the house, backed into a shaded area, and parked.

Pedro dashed for the back door. He ran as fast as he could to meet Joaquin at the place they'd found him some time back. When he got close enough to the place, he slowed down and cautiously walked the rest of the way, looking around to be sure there were no surprises. Once there, Joaquin was nowhere in sight, so Pedro whistled.

Joaquin called out, but didn't show himself, "Hey, *cabrón*, tell me the truth. Did you know?"

"What are you talking about?" Pedro asked.

"Don't you fucking try to lie to me and act like you don't know anything. Did you know who we were working for, and only used me because of my ties to El Warden?" Joaquin, being stern when he asked this, wasn't sure if he was prepared to hear the answer, but was very hopeful that his good friend wasn't just using him.

"*Mira, amigo*, let me tell you. We are friends, and I would do anything for you. I have been nothing but a brother to you. We took you in when we didn't need to, but we did it anyway. My father could've just left you there to die, but instead we helped you and made you a part of the family."

There was an awkward silence after Pedro stopped talking. He slowly started walking around trying to find Joaquin. He called out to him a couple of times, but Joaquin didn't answer. Just as Pedro was going to turn around and walk away, he felt a rope around his neck, and it was pulled really tight, pinching his skin as it gripped him. The tightness of the rope quickly blocked his airflow and stopped the blood from traveling to his brain. Before he knew it, he was pulled just a couple of inches off the ground.

As Pedro was struggling to breathe and stay conscious, Joaquin asked him again, "I am not going to play these games with you. Did you know who we were working for, and did you use me?"

He allowed Pedro to choke for a moment before letting him down just enough so that he could catch his breath and allow some blood to get to his brain. Pedro started coughing, despite the rope still being a little tight around his neck. He was able to get a few fingers under the rope to allow the air and blood to flow.

"Okay, okay…just give me a second. It wasn't like that at first. We were friends… We are friends, and I had no intention of even getting you involved in any of this. But when I heard your story and I told Capitán Alvarez, he made me bring you in. He figured you would be the only way to get close to El Warden. He was putting your name out there in hopes it would reach him. We still haven't seen or heard from their organization, so we don't even know if he's still in play. We know he's out there somewhere; we just don't know where. Capitán Alvarez only intended on using you for your name to lure him out, but you did so good and became the best of all of us, so he couldn't let you go."

Joaquin felt lost at the moment. All the time he trained, thinking he was doing good for the country, and he had been lied to the entire time. The betrayal by the person he thought was his best friend felt like a million knives in the back. He had no idea what to say or think. He finally showed his face and stood right in front of Pedro.

Joaquin stood there looking at him with tear-filled eyes and pure disappointment. Pedro felt the stare as if it were reaching through his chest and squeezing his lungs so he couldn't breathe. The shame he felt after seeing the disappointment in Joaquin's eyes made him stop fighting the rope. He knew he had betrayed him badly and no longer cared if he ended him now.

"Please don't hurt my family. They really like you, and I don't want them to think I'm a terrible person for what I did," Pedro pleaded with Joaquin. "Wait, Joaquin! Before you go, I have something that belongs to you."

Joaquin stopped and turned back to Pedro.

"My left pant pocket. The night you left to go back for it."

Joaquin put his hand into Pedro's pocket and pulled out his father's knife. Tears filled his eyes again, but Joaquin didn't say a word. He just walked away, into the woods, and left Pedro there. As he was leaving, Joaquin let go of the rope, and Pedro fell to the ground, holding his neck and coughing and gasping for air.

Pedro yelled out, "You better not come back through here; they want you dead!"

"Not if I get to them first," Joaquin shouted back.

Knowing that El Warden had already infiltrated the HDM, Joaquin decided he could just sit back, wait for them to attack, and watch them take each other out. He just needed to speed things up. He was able to take a few things from Pedro to help with his plan.

After Joaquin left Pedro, he had found his way behind the men who were in the car following Pedro and easily knocked them out, taking their SAT phones and walkie-talkies. That way, he could hear what they were talking about and when things would be taking place. One of the men was already asleep, so Joaquin only needed to choke one out quietly. He had thought of killing them, but he didn't want to put the HDM on high alert or to have them searching for him. He felt sure that, for fear of what would happen to them, the men wouldn't go back and report that their equipment had been taken from them.

That evening, Pedro walked in as if nothing happened and went about his normal duties. There was a little more commotion than usual, and he stopped someone and asked what was going on.

"They found a mole for El Warden in the ranks here, and now they're questioning him. So far, they found out that they were waiting for that backstabbing *puto* to tell them when our next mission was so that they could ambush us. But, instead, we're going to set up a fake mission and catch those fuckers ourselves. They think they're smarter than us, but they will find out that you can't beat the HDM!"

Pedro was confused a bit because he was still thinking of Joaquin and the look on his face when he walked away from him. This was great news for the HDM because that meant they had been able to reach El Warden with Joaquin's name. Now they had a chance to take him and his organization down. This cheered Pedro up a little because the HDM didn't need to worry about Joaquin anymore since they had El Warden now and were going to make sure he didn't escape this time.

Pedro walked into the briefing room that already had many others inside waiting for Capitán Alvarez. When the captain entered, the room stood up and gave a loud cheer.

He waved, indicating they should settle down, and began by saying, "*Caballeros*, we have been waiting for this day for far too long. This man has escaped so many and has killed many more along the way. After today, he will not be a threat to us or our organization any longer! The HDM will grow and be the most powerful *en todo México*! It's unfortunate that we had a mole in our group, but, thanks to our high-tech surveillance, we were able to find that *hijo de puta*, and he told us everything."

"What about pinche Joaquin?" a voice shouted.

"We no longer need to worry about him since we now have what we were after. If he shows up anywhere, he can be killed on sight, but I highly doubt he will be anywhere near here, considering where I heard he ended up," Capitán Alvarez said, letting out a chuckle.

They continued on about the plans for the mission and how it would be executed. They had someone call from the mole's phone to the man who came to the facility. He was told that there would be a mission happening that night and that it was going to be the biggest one yet.

The message got back to El Warden while he was at dinner, hosting a bunch of friends. When he heard of the plans, he quickly got up and left his party still eating. El Warden was on his phone quickly. He called all his able-bodied men and told them to have everyone ready for that night. There was no way they were going to miss this opportunity to take out their competition.

"I don't care what everyone is doing, *pendejo*. Get them over to the meeting place now. Those cocksuckers are on the move, and we need to take them out now!"

He threw his phone in the car as he got in. El Warden was always impatient and never wanted to hear "can't" or "will try." He only wanted to hear "*sí, señor*" or "right away, *jefe*." Anything less would warrant losing a body part or death.

Back at the facility, Capitán Alvarez had finished briefing the men on the plans, and he walked back to where the mole was being kept. The room was dark and had a single light above where they had the man hanging by his wrists. He had almost no fingernails; they were pulled out during the questioning. He only had one remaining nail on his left pinkie finger. After each nail was pulled off, a rusty nail was stuck in its place. The mole was hanging off the floor with his feet placed in a metal bucket that was covered on top. Inside there were big rats, and the bottom of the bucket had a burner that was controlled by the one asking the questions. He would turn on the burner, and that would cause the rats to try and escape. The only soft place that they could bite and claw their way out of was through the man's feet as he hung there.

As Capitán Alvarez entered the room, a group of six other people were also brought in, including another man, two women, and three younger kids. When the mole saw who they brought in, he became enraged and started thrashing around and screaming. They brought in his family to see the type of man he was. His father, mother, wife, and children were all standing there, looking at the spectacle of what resembled their father/son/husband. They were crying and pleading with Capitán Alvarez to let him go, but he just stood there.

"You really want this type of man in your lives? Scum of the earth, disloyal, and a liar? He doesn't deserve any of you, and you don't need to have this type of filth being called your father. What kind of example is he showing his children? That it is okay to turn on your brothers and work for the enemy? This I cannot allow. It is my duty to make sure that this type of behavior is removed from this land, and people must know it will not be tolerated. So, here's what I'm going to do. I know things may feel like they are too much to bear, or you may feel you cannot take what is going to happen to you, but I will assure you that you can endure a lot more than you think. Buuuuut, in the unfortunate event that you cannot handle this, I will simply allow you to say a safe word. Is that okay with you? How about *pineapple*? That seems like a good word."

The family was then forced to kneel on the floor. The man hanging was yelling, but it was no use since his mouth was covered. The children were holding each other, crying and looking for their mother, and a man was keeping them from moving. The pleading and crying didn't seem to bother the men at all as they took their places behind the family.

"I'm sorry. Are you trying to say something, you fucking piece of shit?" the mole was asked. "I am not a bad man, you *hijo de puta*! Most people would make your family watch you die and send them on their way so that they knew not to ever speak against us or try to double-cross the HDM."

Capitán Alvarez then nodded his head towards the other men, and, all at the same time, they shot the man's family. The mole's scream was muffled by the gag in his mouth as he watched his family fall to the ground.

The one man behind the children had to shoot three times as he was the only one behind them. As the first child was shot, the other two tried to run away, but were met with a bullet that immediately stopped them. Their father looked on in horror as he watched his family be killed. One of the children did not die immediately, and he tried crawling away slowly. The father was shaking and yelling, trying to pull himself free from the bondage that held him in the air. His screaming was quieted once he heard the most horrible sound.

He looked over at the door as a man with a chainsaw walked in and revved it up while walking towards the child who was still trying to crawl away. He stood over the child, and, before touching him with the sharp, rotating blades of the saw, he looked at the mole and said, "This is your fault, *cabrón!*" As he said that, he pushed the spinning blade to the child's neck and buried it until it hit the floor. There was no scream from the child as the chainsaw quickly did what it was meant to do.

The man hanging had to watch as the chainsaw-wielding HDM member, one by one, went to each family member and took off their heads. After finishing with his family, he walked over to the mole with the blades and his face and body covered in blood. "You will die knowing that you killed your family." He then started at the mole's feet and took them off easily with a swipe of the chainsaw. The pain was so excruciating that no sound was even coming out of the hanging man's mouth anymore. The man moved farther up and started cutting the hanging man's legs off at his knees; after the first leg was removed, the mole passed out from the pain. They continued cutting him up until his body was in many different pieces.

The bodies and body parts were left where they fell because the HDM men didn't want to miss their opportunity to capture El Warden. The only things left of the hanging mole were the hands that were still in shackles swinging from the chains. The man with the chainsaw looked around as the room had been splattered with blood and tissue from the constant spinning of the saw's blades.

Another man walked in and said, "*Vámanos*, you sick fuck! I don't know how you have the stomach to do that shit." He was so disgusted by what he saw that he held his hand to his mouth to keep from vomiting.

"Practice from being with your mother, *pendejo*! Only the sickest guy can do her," he replied. He then left the chainsaw and headed to the armory to get ready for that evening. As he walked past the other man, he punched him in the arm after making that remark about his mother, and they both laughed.

About two hours later, the HDM was in place, and they were waiting on El Warden and his men to show up. The evening was warm and humid. The sky was full of clouds that covered the moon, so there was no extra light shining from above.

Joaquin was already there, waiting and watching from a distance, in a spot that he figured they wouldn't go to. From his position, he was able to see the entire meeting area and any vehicle that may come through. Much to his surprise, there was someone running in his direction. He wasn't in a guarded run, and he was alone, so Joaquin figured he was only coming out to gain position. He noticed the long black case on his back, so he knew he was a sniper. He decided to take some cover and see where he would post up and then make a move. Taking him out too early would trigger a warning to the HDM and could sabotage the whole plan.

Joaquin was hoping that both sides would do what they do best and take each other out. El Warden was not very tactical and always wanted to make a grand entrance with loud explosions and guns blazing. He had the manpower and the money to buy expensive guns and pretty much anything that explodes. So when he made an entrance, he made an entrance. The HDM were always tactical and precise with their attacks. They tried to stay quiet and kill with as little noise as possible. Their training and skills were above and beyond what anyone in Mexico had seen. It didn't take long for other organizations in Mexico to take notice and put the HDM on their radar. Capitán Alvarez knew that El Warden would do what he always did, because that's what always worked for him. What he didn't count on was that El Warden knew how the HDM operated and how they conducted their strikes as well, so he prepared for them accordingly.

It was ten minutes past the set time for the meeting. Capitán Alvarez and a few of his men were out in the open, waiting around for El Warden. The rest of his men were in the tree line and waiting for the right moment to strike. The men with Capitán Alvarez started looking at each other after another five minutes, wondering if El Warden was going to show.

"I wonder if he figured this was a trap?" one man asked.

"I don't know; maybe they did since their mole hasn't checked back in," another stated.

All the men gave each other glances from time to time, asking with their eyes, "How much longer are we going to wait?"

Their wait came to an end when Joaquin saw lights coming in the distance. With the sniper in place, Joaquin was still waiting for his moment. He was hiding in a tree above the location where the sniper was. He heard him say over his radio that he was set and ready for the signal. After he stopped speaking, Joaquin jumped down with his knife in his hand and shoved the blade through the back of the sniper's head. He didn't even have time to react before Joaquin fell on him with his blade. The blade went through the top of his head and came out the bottom of his mouth; it could be seen in his open mouth. His eyes began drooping from the nerve that was severed in his brain. There was some twitching in the sniper's legs as Joaquin stood up and pulled him deeper into the woods.

Joaquin returned and took the position that the sniper had intended initially. Looking through the scope, he was able to see closely whom he would strike. He already had it in his mind whom he was going to hit first, and after that he didn't care.

As the cars approached, followed by trucks with fifty-caliber rifles attached to them, the men on the ground drew their weapons, aimed them, and waited for Capitán Alvarez's signal. When the vehicles finally pulled to a stop, the dirt and dust followed behind, making visibility difficult. That's when Capitán Alvarez gave the signal to fire, and the first bullet struck one of the men standing behind the large gun in the truck. His body fell off to the side and hit the ground. Bullets started flying from both directions, and people were falling on both sides.

Joaquin looked on, and it all seemed as if it were unfolding in slow motion as he was searching for his target. He found El Warden; he was sitting in a vehicle, relaxing and watching the onslaught happening before him. Joaquin started to slow his breathing and separating himself from the excitement around him. He closed his eyes and let out another slow breath. He pulled the trigger, knowing he had completed what he set out to do. Joaquin's feelings quickly turned to disappointment when he saw the bullet shatter against the glass and only cause the glass to spider.

"What the fuck! *Pinche* bulletproof glass!!" he yelled out.

This upset Joaquin because he wanted El Warden dead so badly, and it felt like a shot to the gut as he saw El Warden still sitting in his vehicle, laughing. He wasn't sure what else to do after that since he only wanted El Warden dead. He decided to just sit there and watch them kill each other. He picked one off here and there to help even the odds, but didn't get involved too much.

Capitán Alvarez then signaled the other men that were in the forest to come to their aid. What he didn't know was that El Warden had anticipated this type of an assault, so he only made them think he would be his usual self. What Capitán Alvarez didn't know is that El Warden had his men go into the woods and slaughter the HDM men before they had a chance to even call for help. The massacre didn't take long, and when Capitán Alvarez realized that he had been beaten, he ordered his men to surrender. There weren't very many men left from the HDM, so El Warden's men gathered them all together and surrounded them. El Warden then stepped out of his vehicle, knowing that they were no longer a threat. He walked over to Capitán Alvarez and the other men, who were on their knees.

Joaquin couldn't believe he had another opportunity. He began to slow his breathing again and closed his eyes to adjust his vision. He could feel and hear his heart pounding as loud as a drum. His heart rate began to slow down. When he opened his eyes again, he put the small cross hairs from the scope on El Warden's head. Joaquin couldn't hear what was being said, but he could see El Warden laughing and pointing a gun to Capitán Alvarez's head. More words were exchanged, but Joaquin didn't care what was said because he was focused. A single shot rang out, and Capitán Alvarez fell back.

This was it for Joaquin. He could not have asked for a clearer shot. He closed his eyes again, and this time he saw his mother and Cati. All the trouble and pain this man had caused to so many people rolled through Joaquin's mind. The hatred he felt for El Warden was just so great that Joaquin wished he could've done something sooner to prevent El Warden from destroying so many other lives. In Joaquin's mind, Cati was smiling at him, as always, and his mother was holding him as a young child. So many emotions in one split second. His heartbeat had become so slow he could barely hear it now.

Joaquin opened his eyes while holding his breath and gently squeezed the trigger. The shot roared down that field, and, before it hit, Joaquin felt a heavy burden lift off his shoulders, knowing he had avenged his loved ones' killer. He felt at peace in an instant and had no more hate as that bullet found its mark.

El Warden's head opened up as his left eye seemed to have exploded outwards, across one of his men's face. For an instant, El Warden just stood standing as if nothing happened; then, his body slowly collapsed to the ground.

This caused an uproar, and El Warden's men pointed their focus in Joaquin's direction. Joaquin didn't want to sit around and wait to see what those men would do next, so he jumped up and ran into the forest, trying to get as far away as possible. No words could describe the feelings Joaquin was having as he ran through those woods. He was able to take down two organizations at the same time and kill the man who had taken everything from him. Even though he was running for his life, he felt wonderful knowing he did what he had to do for his family.

Chapter 11

Land of the Free

As they pulled up to the facility that should be the final stop before being sent back to Honduras, Joaquin felt a sense of achievement as he looked back on all that he accomplished and went through. He wouldn't wish any of it on his worst of enemies, even though he knew one in particular deserved it.

"Okay, *caballeros*, I know it was a long ride, and we thank you for being patient, but let's get you off this bus and inside so you can eat, shower, and find you a nice, warm bed to sleep in."

This caused a few of the men to clap and tell the officer thank you for being nice to them and not treating them like animals. The officer unlocked the chains that had them secured to the floor by their feet. The men were then instructed to head off the bus and line up outside, along the bus, and wait for further instructions.

They were then called out one at a time by their names, and as they were called, the men slowly made their way to an area in front of the doors to go inside. Tired from the long bus ride, having to waddle because their legs were restrained was beginning to frustrate some of the men. The ones in the red-and-orange uniforms who were seated in the front seemed to be more frustrated. They started making smart remarks, and when the officers told them to be quiet, their response was, "Fuck you, I'm tired," or "How about you make me shut the fuck up." The officers had enough restraint to not engage with these men as it always led to someone being sent to solitary.

Joaquin stepped off the bus; he could smell the exhaust from the bus and feel the heat coming off the tires as he walked past them. He was looking at the men who were giving the officers a hard time and made eye contact with one of them. The man had many tattoos on his body, but the one that stood out was the giant letter on his forehead.

He looked back at Joaquin and shouted, "What the fuck you looking at, old man? No one was talking to you; move along before you get handled."

Joaquin just shook his head, looked away, and found his place where the officers wanted them to stand.

Group by group, they were escorted into the building since there was a double door and not everyone could fit into the corridor between the two doors. Once inside, there were officers directing them where to go and which holding cell to enter. Before they went into the cell, two officers took off their restraints. The men felt so relieved to have the restraints removed from their wrists and ankles. Many walked away rubbing their wrists and stretching since they hadn't been able to raise their hands above their shoulders all day. They started forming a line by the toilets as many needed to relieve themselves.

"Joaquin Tejirina Navarez," an officer called out, and Joaquin moved forward with that group waiting by the door.

Once inside, the restraints were removed, and they told Joaquin to go in the holding cell with the red-and-orange-uniformed men. As he walked in, the other men stopped talking and stared at him, trying to figure out who he was.

The young man who yelled at Joaquin earlier said, "Don't come in here starting shit, old man. If you got something to say or do, you better bring it. You can't be staring at people like that unless you about something."

Joaquin just ignored him and walked around, away from them. He was rubbing his wrist and thinking that he only needed to be here a couple more days, and then he was going back to Honduras. The men started talking amongst themselves, and Joaquin kept to himself while the whole intake process proceeded.

There were several officers at a large desk, and they had computers in front of them. Five at a time, the men were escorted out and told to find an open seat in front of an officer. The officer would then ask for a name and date of birth to verify identity. They would then compare it to the name on the paperwork they had. Once verified, an officer would go and find the personal belongings that the detainee had brought with them; those were bagged and tagged with the detainee's name and date of birth. The officer would then inventory the personal belongings and ask other questions that were required for the process. The questions were mainly about where they were from and potential medical issues. They started with the men in Joaquin's cell first as they tended to be the more problematic if they stayed too long together. So, to avoid those issues, they just checked them in first. After they completed the check-in process, the detainees were shown to the showers and were given fresh clothing before being taken back to the holding cell, awaiting being moved to the main rooms.

When Joaquin's turn was up, he found a seat open next to an officer who was checking in females. She was the only one checking them in as there were only ten of them in a cell by themselves; they had been there since before Joaquin's group arrived. He went to sit down and noticed that the woman who was sitting next to him seemed very sad; there was something off about her. She was very dirty as she had probably been walking in the woods for weeks without a shower. Her hair was very dirty and oily, but what caught Joaquin's eye the most was that her hair seemed as if it were moving.

Joaquin hesitated a quick second before sitting down and looked over at the officer. The officer then looked at the lady sitting there, and when Joaquin looked back at her, he saw a tick crawl over her face and back into her hair. This caused the officer to jump from her chair and let out a sharp yelp. She walked away, and another officer had to come take over. Joaquin was slow to sit down and felt sorry for that woman who had her hair infested with lice and ticks that ran freely on her face. What really surprised Joaquin was that she didn't even flinch when the tick ran across her forehead.

Joaquin was running for what seemed like all night. He had already mapped out an escape route to make it difficult for El Warden's men to find him. There was a creek he ran with for about two miles before cutting over into the woods. The splashing from the water hitting him felt refreshing as it was a very warm evening. He continued to run until he was close to the Rio Grande de Santiago River. He felt so much lighter running this evening. Even though he was still running for his life, he knew that not even those men after him could take away the joy he felt. He only needed to stop twice to be sure he was running in the correct direction. As soon as he found his bearings, he was off again.

It was already morning when he reached the Santiago River, and he approached a man who was tending to his boat and nets. The man only had on some pants that were torn at the calf. He had a *Virgen de Guadalupe* cloth medallion around his neck. His hair was long, but not tied back.

"Hola, señor, ¿puede usted ayudar me?" Joaquin asked.

To which, he replied, "Depends on what type of help you need. Based on the heavy breathing and the type of clothes you are wearing, you need more than just help." The man didn't stop working on his net as he answered Joaquin.

"Well, yes, you're right. I am in trouble, but I only need to be taken upriver and dropped off where the migrants get on the train," Joaquin said.

"*Pues*, you are in luck today, because I am actually having to ride that way. Only problem is that gas isn't cheap, and I still need to fill up," the man eagerly said with a grin on his face.

Joaquin reached into his pocket and pulled out an American twenty-dollar bill, and the man's smile grew even bigger.

"Well, for that much, I can be your taxi all day!" he said as he quickly grabbed the bill before Joaquin changed his mind. "*Vamos, amigo*, we must get going if you are to catch that train."

Joaquin jumped into the boat, and the man carefully went to the engine and pulled on the string twice, until the puttering of that small engine sprang to life. Smoke and the smell of burning gas filled Joaquin's nostrils as the man grabbed the handle to the engine and revved it up by turning it. He then lowered the engine into the water and turned the handle as far as it could go, and then they began moving. It was no speedboat, but at least he was putting some distance between him and those men after him.

The ride up the river was not very long, and there was no conversation between the two men as the noise from the small engine was too loud. Joaquin was able to calm his body down from the long run he had that evening. He was beginning to feel the soreness in his legs and back from the dehydration. He had a bag with a large bottle of water and began drinking as much as he could. He offered some to his taxi driver, but he refused by shaking his head and putting up a hand.

After about an hour, the man started slowing down, and a look of concern came over him. "*Mira, señor,* I don't know who you are and what kind of trouble you are in, but I'm looking upriver, and I noticed several boats are getting checked by men."

Shit! Joaquin thought to himself.

"I have never seen men like that on this river, checking other boats, so I can only assume they're looking for you," he told Joaquin.

"What will you do? I don't want you to get in trouble because of me," Joaquin said.

"You have been nice to me, and you don't come across as a bad man, so I am going to help you. You are going to have to hide, though."

Joaquin gave him a confused look because the boat they were in barely had enough room for the two of them, let alone a place for him to hide. "Where am I supposed to hide, if you don't mind me asking?" he asked with a slightly sarcastic tone.

The man smiled again and said, "Things in life aren't always as they seem, *mi amigo.* I need you to stand up and move towards the front of the boat."

Joaquin moved the two feet until he was in the front part of the boat, and the man moved the board he was sitting on. It was attached to some of the floor that opened up to the bottom part of the boat. It was not very big, but big enough to fit a full-grown man. Joaquin looked at the man, and the man quickly replied, "Hey, I'm not questioning you and what you do, so don't question me and what I do."

Joaquin smiled and held his hands up as if to say, "Okay, okay, I'm not judging here."

Joaquin figured this man was a smuggler. What he smuggled, he wasn't entirely sure, but today it was going to be Joaquin, so he was okay with that. He quickly lay down in the small area, but still had plenty of room on his sides and for his feet. You couldn't tell from the outside that it had a false bottom because of how small the boat was, and that's what made it more convincing. Being that he was a fisherman, Joaquin figured he used fishing as a cover because it didn't smell as if he put fish in this compartment of the boat. Either way, he was thankful he chartered him to take him upriver, given that he was being searched for.

"Don't worry, *amigo*, we'll get you through this. *Mi Lucinda* hasn't failed me yet," he said as he revved the engine again then patted it, as if petting a dog.

Joaquin smiled and then gave him a thumbs-up as the man replaced the seat and covered the loose plank with flooring. He then heard the small engine rev louder, and he could feel the water through the floor where he was lying. There was a little bit of water in there, but not so much to worry about, as water does get into boats at times. He lay there praying that there wouldn't be any reason for them to stop and search the boat. As they got closer to where they were checking the boats, Joaquin could hear them asking questions to the other boat riders.

When it was their turn, he heard one ask, *"Hola, buenos días,* we are asking if anyone has seen a man that was dressed in clothing that is typical around these areas, and if he may have asked for a ride from anyone."

Joaquin listened quietly and tried not to move as the questioning was going on.

"Not today. I haven't seen anyone out of the ordinary, besides you guys. What did this man do? Should we be concerned if we do see him?" the boat driver asked.

"That's none of your concern at the moment; we only want to find him and speak with him" was the response. "Can we check your boat?" he asked.

"Mira, señor, I don't mind if you check my boat, but you can see that I barely fit in this boat, and it's empty. I really don't see where you think anyone can hide in this little thing."

One of the other men smacked the back of the head of the man asking questions. "Yeah, *pendejo!* Where do you think he's going to hide? Hurry up and go, *señor."*

With that, Joaquin heard the two men from the other boat argue a little about the questions and why did he smack him like that as Joaquin's boat drove off with the little engine squealing up the river. After about ten minutes, the boat slowed and the man removed the seat and flooring again. With the same smile, he looked at Joaquin and said, *"Ya llegamos, amigo.* We're here."

Joaquin slid out of the compartment and slowly looked around. When he saw that there was no one else around, he stood up and looked towards the shore.

The man told him that he just needed to continue on that road for about five miles, and then he'd see the train tracks. Follow them for as long as he needed to until a train came by. "The train doesn't move very fast, so you should be okay to jump on and go where you need to," the man said as he jumped out of the boat and pulled it to shore.

Joaquin jumped out, shook the man's hand, and gave him another twenty-dollar bill.

This caused the man to smile again. He reached into a box in the front of the boat and pulled out some clothes. He handed them to Joaquin and told him, "These belonged to *mi hermano*. He was much bigger than me, so they should fit you, no problem."

"*Muchas gracias, señor*. I really appreciate all of your help," Joaquin told him as he walked off, down that road.

As Joaquin was walking, he would occasionally look around to be sure that no one was coming in his direction or following him. He had changed his clothes so that he could blend in amongst the people. The clothes had a slight fishy smell to them, and they did fit him a little bigger than he expected. *Beggars can't be choosers*, he thought to himself. Joaquin couldn't believe that a stranger like him helped him out without any question. He figured he didn't want any attention on himself since he was a smuggler. Bringing unwanted attention is an easy way to get caught.

Along the road, he passed a few other locals, and as he was getting closer to the train, he noticed several other people walking in groups with bags and backpacks. Many people gathered along a certain area near the train tracks, and Joaquin only assumed that is where they made their attempt to jump on the train. Many men traveled alone or in groups. Women traveled together in smaller groups, many of them with children. While other couples stayed close together so they wouldn't be split up. The looks on their faces seemed of good spirit, even not knowing what lay ahead for them. They only knew that they must find a way to provide for their families. Several were sad because they had to leave their family, despite hearing the stories of what happened to those who went before them. For many of these people, it would be their first attempt to leave. Unfortunately, many wouldn't make it or ever return to their families.

Tears of joy and sadness swept through the crowd as the sound of the train's horn could be heard for miles and miles. Those who were lying around, waiting, quickly got up and collected their things, and their voices started getting louder. They started saying their good-byes to the loved ones who came to see them off, and others began yelling, *"¡El tren está llegando!"* The train is coming.

Joaquin was waiting and looking at all who had gathered to try to get on this moving train. He knew he wouldn't have any issue, but many of the others—women or older people and children—he wasn't so sure if they'd make it.

As the train was approaching, a commotion started not far from where the people were standing. Joaquin noticed gunmen pushing their way through the crowd and looking for someone. They only seemed to be going after the men who appeared to be around Joaquin's age. Joaquin tried not to appear startled or make any sudden movements as the men were getting closer to him. He decided that he did not want anyone to get hurt if they found him out, so he slowly started to walk away, trying to avoid eye contact with any of those men. Since he was not watching where he was going, he accidentally bumped into a lady and a child.

She yelled at him, *"Ten cuidado, cabrón!"*

This caused others to turn and look at Joaquin as he started to walk away a little faster. The men looked his way and weren't going to say anything, but one of the three men noticed the boots Joaquin was wearing and knew that those weren't boots anyone around this area could afford or would be wearing.

"¡Espera! ¡No te muevas, pendejo!" one of the men yelled out, which caused Joaquin to start running away from the large crowd.

He didn't think those men would fire at him in the large crowd, but he quickly found out that they didn't care who was in the way. The three men opened fire at Joaquin, and he heard a couple of bullets zip right past his ear. Joaquin was trying to avoid this because he knew that if he didn't get shot, others could get hit by the stray bullets.

The crowd started dispersing in all directions, trying not to get hit by the men shooting. A couple of bullets that missed Joaquin hit a man running next to him. One in the shoulder and the other to the back of the neck. He immediately fell to the ground and was not able to move as the bullet hit his spinal cord and came out the front of his throat, leaving a big hole. The blood poured out, and he started suffocating on his own blood. Another bullet hit a man in the leg then ricocheted and hit a little girl in the stomach. The mother of that little girl fell to the ground with her daughter, crying as the little girl lay there motionless. As Joaquin turned to move away from more of the innocent people, a woman was struck in the head, and her husband still held on to her as he dragged her to safety. Her lifeless body had blood and brain particles all over her chest and his shoulder as he carried her while her legs dragged on the ground. Others were hit in the arm or legs as Joaquin was trying to run away from the crowd to draw the bullets away from the people. Everywhere he ran, the people seemed to run in that direction.

The bullets stopped coming when he was too far for the men to shoot. The three men took off running after him and followed him in the direction of the road that Joaquin had come from. There was a wooded area there, and he needed to get cover from these men so they couldn't shoot anyone else.

The train made its way down the track and blew its horn as people started forming again to climb aboard. Despite what just happened, there was no stopping some from getting on that train. Many had started running towards the train and trying to get a head start to jump on, while others stayed and waited for the train to come to them.

In the wooded area, Joaquin found a spot from which he knew he could hold the men off or make a stand if the men tried to come after him. He stayed as quiet as possible as the men came in together, walking side-by-side. Joaquin only had his father's knife in hand. He could hear the train getting closer and closer, and the more time he spent here, the bigger chance he had of missing that train. He needed to act quickly and get back to the train.

The three men were looking around for Joaquin, and he was patiently waiting for them to pass where he was hiding. He only needed a few more feet, and they would be close enough for him to strike. His breathing slowed, and his heartbeat was drowned out as he could hear their breathing and smell the cheap cologne that one of them was wearing. He jumped out and grabbed the barrel of the gun from the man who was closest to him, and he kicked the other one in the middle in the chest hard enough to send him flying into the third man farthest from him. After the kick, he pulled the man closer to him by the gun and drove the knife under his chin, pulled it out, and stabbed him just behind the head into his upper back along his spine. He then stopped the man he'd kicked to the ground from standing up by breaking his leg at the knee. He was able to grab him by the neck with one hand and turn him around with his arm around his neck and walk him towards the third man who shot twice and hit his partner in the chest. Joaquin then pushed the man he had in his arms into the remaining man and tackled him as he pushed his partner away from him. Joaquin's knife found the man's belly, and he pulled it from one side to the other before burying the knife in the man's right eye. Joaquin stood up and looked at the man holding his broken leg. He picked up a gun from the ground and shot him twice in the chest and once in the head. Then, before running for the train, he dropped the gun while looking around to be sure that no one else was there.

The train had already passed the area where people had been waiting, and they started running and jumping onto the train. Those who made it on first helped those trying to get on. Joaquin ran as fast as he could to make the train as it was not very long. As he was trying to make his way to the train, he saw the many people who were injured and the others who died from the men's open fire just moments before. He wanted to stop and help them, but he couldn't stay, knowing that other men would come looking as well. Thankfully, no one really knew that he was the one they were after since so many people were running; after he'd run to the woods, no one saw him kill the men.

The train was moving along and didn't seem to care that people were trying to jump on it for a ride. Joaquin saw all the people who had already jumped on and noticed that many of the older people and women with their children still were trying to get on. He was almost getting there as he saw that the end of the train was getting closer. He knew he couldn't stop; he needed to run faster to catch this beast. Once he finally reached it, he was trying to time his speed to run and jump at the same time. Several cars ahead, a group of older men were running, and one tripped and caused the other men with him to fall as well. A woman had been carrying her child and trying to grab ahold of the hand of her husband, but could not keep up, so she stopped running. There were a few younger girls in front of Joaquin getting ready to jump; one of them made it easily, but her friend lost her footing. Joaquin was there and grabbed her so she didn't fall and pretty much threw her into the open car door. She was able to grab on to her friend, who pulled her in the rest of the way. This caused Joaquin to lose some speed so he needed to retime his jump.

At the car in front of him, he saw this man push others out of his way so that he could jump ahead of them. The people he pushed fell down, and it upset Joaquin to see the man do that to others. The man was getting ready to jump, and he tripped on a railroad tie spike, but he was already high enough that he was able to grab the handle of the car door. He was trying to pull himself in, and his feet were dragging, but he was having difficulty since he didn't have enough upper-body strength. He tried pushing off with his feet, but they kept dragging as the train was moving. He attempted to put his feet somewhere under the train to get his footing so he could pull himself up. He was able to step on a hard surface, and when he went to pull himself up, he slipped. This caused him to swing farther under the train, and his foot got caught in the wheel of the train. The man screamed in agony as he was pulled under and both legs got trapped in the wheels. It only took a second; the wheels pulled his legs, and when he hit the tracks, the train ran over his legs, cutting them clean off. The blood painted the wheels as his body rolled off to the side and down the hill. Others looked on with grief and amazement at what they just witnessed.

Joaquin thought to himself, "*Ándale, cabrón,* that's what you get, fucker." With that last thought, he jumped on and was able to help a few others get on because the farther they went, the people could no longer keep up. They would have to wait for the next train and try again.

After that stretch of craziness with getting on the train, those who made it on began to calm down and find their own places to sit within and on top of the cars. They were happy and congratulated each other, and the families and friends who stayed behind cheered them on as the train shrank smaller and smaller, until it was out of view.

Joaquin walked around looking for a place to sit, and when he passed by a couple whom he helped on, they moved over and made room for him to sit. They were a husband and wife, and they were headed to California to meet with a cousin of hers who had a job waiting for them. The husband had already made this trip once and was doing it again, but with his wife this time. Joaquin sat down, and they thanked him again for helping them. The husband told him that it would be about ten hours before their next stop.

Joaquin figured that now would be the best time to finally get some rest since it had been almost two days since he had any. He looked around and saw everyone as they laid their heads on each other and settled in for a long ride ahead. The car was full, and it didn't leave much room to stretch your legs. He closed his eyes feeling at ease, knowing that he was that much closer to getting to America, but also feeling alone, knowing those he loved were not going to be with him.

Joaquin was awakened by the screeching of the train wheels as it was making a long turn. He hadn't any idea how long he was asleep, but it was dark when he woke up. He was startled to see that the car was completely empty. He looked around and saw no one. Standing up, he walked towards the door and saw that the train was still moving, but no one was in the car he was in. He listened to see if he could hear anyone on top of the car, but there was no one. When he turned, he saw a hand holding on to the handle of the car door, and he could hear someone yelling for help. He ran to them quickly and grabbed the hand. When he poked his head out there, he saw Cati.

She screamed, "Joaquin! Help me, Joaquin. I can't hold on!"

When he realized it was her, he pulled harder to bring her in. He was able to finally pull her up and noticed, as she stood up, that she was pregnant. He was very confused because he didn't know how she got out there in the first place.

He heard another voice yelling for him on the other side of the car, and he saw another hand holding on to the handle. He reached for that hand, looked out, and found his mother hanging on for dear life. "¡Ayúdame, Joaquín! ¡Por favor!" she yelled out. The train started moving much faster, and her body was hitting against the side of the train. Joaquin grabbed ahold of her wrists and pulled as hard as he could and was able to pull her into the car.

The shock that he felt when he saw his mother and Cati was overwhelming, and he just held them so tightly. He had no idea how they got there or why, but he was glad he could see them. He held them for what seemed like an eternity, until he finally pulled away and asked them, "What are you doing here, or should I ask how did you get here?"

"What do you mean, what are we doing here? You are the one that left us Joaquin!" his mother said in a stern tone. He turned and looked at them both, and they returned the questioning look to him. "I was alone, and I had no one to protect me," she continued. "I waited by the pillar for you, and you never came back. Why wouldn't you come back for me, Joaquin?"

"I loved you and wanted to be with you forever, and even have children with you," Cati said as her eyes filled with tears. "Why would you leave me like that? I thought you loved me!"

"What are you both talking about? I do love you, and I would never leave you!" Joaquin said with concern in his voice. He pulled away from them out of frustration and because he wasn't sure why they were telling him these things. When he looked back at Cati, he looked down at her stomach and asked, "How did this happen? Is this mine?"

"No, when you left me, I was devastated, and I was all alone. I didn't have anyone, and I wasn't able to eat or do anything because you left," Cati said with tears falling steadily down her cheeks.

"Why do you keep saying I left you? You know I was taken away by your uncle and his men," Joaquin said.

"Well, that's not what my *tio* says. He says you didn't love me and that he is the only one that will love me and that he would never leave me the way you did. So, to show me how much he loves me, he's giving me a baby."

Joaquin had no words for what he just heard. He backed away out of disbelief. As he was backing up, someone grabbed his shoulder and turned him around. His eyes widened as he looked at the distorted face of El Warden. The left side of his face was covered in blood, and his eye was gone from where it was shot out from behind. He had a big smile on his face. Joaquin looked away and saw that the train was moving so fast that you couldn't make out what was outside.

He looked back at El Warden, who said, "You thought you could get rid of me, *cabrón*? I am everywhere, and no one can escape me! I even made sure that Cati will give you a part of me." He laughed again.

Joaquin was so angry that he swung at him, but when he punched him, El Warden turned into a mist of some sort and disappeared. Joaquin quickly turned back to Cati and his mother, and they were standing there looking at him. Joaquin went to grab Cati's hand, and when he did, she started turning into a charred corpse, eventually disintegrating into ash and floating away. Joaquin did not understand what was going on, and his heart was beating faster than it ever had. He then reached for his mother, and before she could reach back for him, a vulture came and took her away.

He yelled and tried to reach for them—

Joaquin was shaken awake by the husband of the couple he helped onto the train. He was sweating from the anxiety caused by the dream, and his heart was pounding out of his chest. He couldn't believe that he was still dreaming about El Warden.

"We're coming to the stop, *señor*," the husband told Joaquin. "From here, we walk about ten miles to catch another train. That one should be stopped, so no need to jump on a moving train this time."

Joaquin was still shaken from his dream and was only partially paying attention to what was being said. He just nodded his head and stood up to get off the train. He had fallen asleep long enough for his muscles to tighten up, and he felt every sore muscle in his body as he was standing and walking towards the car door. He had to stop a moment because he had gotten a spasm in his lower back, and it shot all the way down his legs. Shaking it off, he continued towards the door, grabbed the handle, and jumped out. After looking around for a moment, he helped a few others down off the train.

The large group of people from the train started to walk in the same direction. Joaquin had no idea where he was going, so he just followed along with them. He looked around at the others and saw that many were already tired after that train ride, and, based on what he was told, they still had a long way to go.

Married couples obviously walked together, while many of the women traveling alone bunched together so they could help each other. As they started off on the ten-mile walk, Joaquin just stayed by himself and didn't speak with anyone. He noticed several groups of men walking together, while many men walked alone. The younger kids stayed close to their parents, but they would try to walk together so that they could keep each other entertained throughout the journey. The parents didn't mind, so long as they stayed within eyesight. The evening was warm, and the mosquitos had found their meals for the next ten miles or so. Despite it being a large group, the pace was pretty quick. There were a few who had already made this trip; they set the pace and led the way.

During the walk, the group had become larger as they got closer to the next train ride. Many of the travelers were already showing signs of fatigue and agitation. The older people fell way back since they could no longer keep up. Joaquin noticed many of the people staying away from him and occasionally whispering amongst themselves as they moved from his path. He only assumed that they recognized him as the one the armed men were chasing. He decided he needed to change things up so he didn't appear too noticeable amongst the others.

Along the walk, there were some areas where people were selling food and water to those who were traveling. Since the travelers didn't have much money, the vendors weren't trying to sell the food for too much. They knew that they were traveling, and they needed to eat or drink. Roasted corn, egg and bean taquitos, and plenty of fruits were available for them to enjoy. Many of the vendors would give food to the mothers with children.

Joaquin was able to find someone who had some clothing and a cap for him to wear. He gave the man a five-dollar bill, and the man was very grateful. After changing, Joaquin continued to walk. The group that was keeping a certain pace had gone ahead, so he knew he needed to speed up to catch them. Along the way, he noticed three men walking behind this couple. One of the men had shoulder-length hair that looked as if he hadn't washed the grease out of it in a long time. His mustache was really thin, and it appeared that he couldn't grow a beard. Another was shaved, and he had tattoos all over his body and face. He wore a jersey-style shirt. He had been doing many types of drugs because he was very thin, and many of his teeth were rotten. The last man had really long hair, gold-capped front teeth, and a missing hand. The couple held each other very closely and were trying to speed up, but it was difficult since they were holding one another. They weren't even looking up; they kept their heads down as they were walking.

It was well past midnight when they made it to the next stop, and everyone was tired. The group that made it first was not the same size from when they left the train, but they were slowly making their way there. It was very quiet when they arrived as most of those who were already there were sleeping. Only a few were walking around as if keeping an eye on everyone. Every ten minutes or so, another small group of people would come down that road exhausted and needing to stop. Joaquin was not as tired, but he was very sweaty from the long walk, and it was very warm. As he was walking around, he overheard a few men saying that the train wasn't due to show up until the morning, which was a few hours away. Many of the people had already been there for many hours. They said others didn't care to wait and decided to just walk and see how far they could make it. Joaquin decided to find a spot near a run-down shack and leaned up against it to rest. He wasn't very tired since he had slept for that long time during the first train ride. He just sat there looking around at those who were waiting patiently and seeing everyone as they arrived. The number of people at this station was greater than those waiting for the first train. This must be a more centralized area for many of those looking to escape.

Joaquin noticed that couple again as they finally arrived; the three men were still following behind them. The couple tried to walk away from them, but the men just lingered close-by. An eerie feeling came over Joaquin as he again took notice of the men, and he knew what their intentions were. He kept watching as the men looked around from time to time to see if anyone was paying attention. When they felt certain that no one was, two of the men went towards the couple and grabbed the man, while the other man grabbed the woman. They dragged them both behind a smaller building that looked abandoned.

That prompted Joaquin to get up. He moved quickly and made sure that the men couldn't see or hear him coming. The woman was screaming as the man pulled her by the hair and neck. She was clawing and kicking, trying to get away, because she knew what was going to happen. She had no way of know that Joaquin was not going to let those men have their way. He looked for the husband and saw that two men were holding him down and forcing him to watch what the man with all the tattoos was about to do to his wife. The man with a missing hand had his arm around the husband's neck, forcing him to keep it up as the assault on his wife progressed. The man screamed and pleaded for the men to quit, but they didn't care to listen to his cries. They laughed and spit at him.

One of the men even told him, "Don't worry, *puto*; you're next!"

The man with the tattoos found a place to throw the woman on the ground. She tried to crawl away, but he grabbed her by the ankles and pulled her back. He slapped her hard in the face, which caused her to be stunned for a moment. He then tore her dress open and held her hands over her head. She was screaming and crying to let her go, but the man wasn't listening. He forced a kiss on her lips. She could smell the fish he ate earlier, and she bit him. He pulled away and felt blood in his mouth from the bite. She tried to get away again, and he just laughed and continued to do what he set out to do. He pulled off her underwear, tearing them.

The shock of being exposed so brutally caused the woman to despair. Her underwear was all she had as a barrier, but now that it was gone, she felt defeated. There was no stopping this man, and she wanted to just die instead of feeling this man take her this way. *How can my husband look at me again? Will he think less of me? Is there a chance he will not want to be with me anymore?* These questions were flying through her mind as that man was getting ready to force his way into her. She closed her eyes because she didn't want to see the evil that man had on his face. She felt him rip her blouse, exposing her breast. Just when she felt him lean closer to her, she felt his grip on her hands ease.

She opened her eyes and saw the blade of a knife being pulled out of his neck and then plunge back in three or four times. It happened so quickly she almost didn't see it. With each piercing of the blade, it caused blood to spill out and hit her in the face and chest.

Joaquin pulled the man off her and tossed him to the side, allowing him to choke on his own blood and suffocate on it. His two partners didn't even have a chance to react before Joaquin was grabbing one by the neck and stabbing the other in the chest. After the knife went into the one's chest, he pulled it out and, with the same momentum, dragged it across the other's neck.

The husband quickly ran to his wife, who was rubbing the blood off her face and trying to cover up. Joaquin didn't stay to see if they were fine.

When the couple looked back towards Joaquin, he was gone. As they came from behind that building, they saw Joaquin sitting in the same place he was when they initially passed him. Joaquin just looked at them as they passed by, and they said nothing, only held each other close and walked off as fast as they could. A little commotion stirred up as other people saw the woman with blood all over her and her torn clothes. There were a few people who ran over behind the building where the woman was assaulted, and they came back in a hurry, confirming that what she said actually happened.

Joaquin just sat there, not saying anything and only trying to relax for the ride they were about to take. It was an hour before the train was scheduled to arrive, and several trucks with men and guns pulled up and surrounded the area. Everyone was ordered to gather around to hear what was going to be said. The people who had gathered around the assaulted couple took their time gathering as they were still tending to them and making sure that they were okay.

"Señores y señoras, mucho gusto en este buen día," a man standing on the hood of one of the trucks stated in a loud but calm tone. Thank you for all being here on this fine day. *"¡Hola! Me llamo Flaco.* If you could all just give me a moment of your time as the train is due to arrive shortly. I would hate to be the reason you miss your train." Flaco was a large man who had his belly hanging out the bottom of his shirts. He was drenched in sweat and wheezed with every other word when he took a deep breath. As the people were all gathered finally, he continued, "Look, I know and understand that many of you have nothing to offer and that the reason you're getting on this train is to make it up north so you can live the American dream. I too have made this journey, and I am living that dream now. Unfortunately, you are on my land, and, even though the train doesn't belong to me, someone has to clean up after you have left here. Cleaning up costs money, and you can't just expect me to pay for this all by myself, especially since I'm being gracious enough to allow you on my land."

The people started mumbling amongst themselves and questioning what was going on. The men who had led the way worked with Flaco, and they knew to lead them to this area where the train stopped.

"Again, I know most of you have no money to give, but what I do see amongst you is plenty of payment that does not require money."

The people started looking around at each other, and many began walking away. The men with the guns cocked them, loading a round in each chamber. The sound caused everyone to freeze in place as the armed men aimed the guns at the people. Joaquin knew there was no way out of this with so many armed men. There were too many people huddled together, and if he tried getting away, it would be a bloodbath.

"Now, people, I am trying to be nice and be civil about this. I need everyone to be still and not leave. As you can see, my men here are a little nervous, and their fingers tend to tremble when they are. You really don't want to see what happens when their fingers tremble. Like I said, I don't want to be the reason you are late for your train ride."

A silence fell over the group, and many of the women and children gathered closer together. Joaquin felt helpless and wanted to figure out a way to help everyone, but he was only one man with a knife, and all these men had guns. He quickly realized that they weren't there for him, but to rob these people of whatever they could since they were claiming rights to this land. The people were becoming scared and unsure about what the men were going to do.

Flaco kept on with his proposal. "So this is what I am willing to do for you. I will allow you all to come up, one by one, and give me half of whatever money you have on you."

This caused the people to yell and become very upset, and they all started pleading for him to not be this unfair. The noise was getting too loud, and Flaco was unable to finish what he was saying. There was a younger man in the front of the group, and he was yelling at Flaco, which caused him to hold up his hand. When he did that, one of the armed men shot the young man in the leg, making him fall to the ground and hold his wound.

"Now, see, I did not want this to have to turn into demonstrating who is in charge here, but if you only want to yell and not listen, then we can have a completely different conversation. I don't believe I was asking for a discussion. In fact, I was telling you what I am willing to allow you to do for me."

The people again quieted down out of fear.

Flaco continued, "So, as I was saying, I will allow you to give me half of your money. If you do not have any money on you, and you are a man or woman traveling alone, you will be given a small package that you will carry with you and take to the next stop. All of you will be traveling together in a separate car so that my men can keep an eye on you and so you don't try and steal the package or run away. You won't know who they are because they are already amongst you, so you can't avoid them. Upon arriving at the stop, there will be other men waiting for you to deliver these packages. You will then be given another package that you will take over to the American side. Once there, you will hand over that package, be given some money for your troubles, and sent on your way. See, that isn't too bad now, is it? For those of you with children and no money, you will also be given a package to take with you. All of you will go through the same process as the others. There will be no need to have my men with you because we will be holding your children and waiting for you on the other side."

This caused a big uproar; the parents held on to their children and yelled that they would not let them go. The yelling grew louder, and Flaco nodded his head to one of the armed men. He began shooting into the air. The crowd quieted down, and the women and children began crying amongst themselves.

"Okay, everyone, I'm guessing you weren't taking me seriously when I said that this isn't a request."

When he said that, the young man on the ground and holding his leg was shot in the head, and the crowd looked on in horror as the young man's blood poured out onto the ground as he lay there motionless with his eyes still open.

"So, I'm guessing, now that I have your attention, we can get past the part where you assumed I'm asking if you want to do this." Flaco then ordered them to get into the two groups so that they could start paying or collecting their packages. The train whistle blew, and Flaco told everyone to hurry. "We need to hurry, everyone. The train will take about an hour to completely stop, and then you'll have another hour before it takes off again. The faster we get this done, the faster you can be on your way and into the land of opportunities."

Joaquin decided to just go along with what they were telling them to do, so that no one would get hurt and he didn't get shot. One by one, they were forced to empty their pockets and bags to see if they had any money. They complied because of the men pointing the large-caliber rifles at them and because they wanted to get to America. During this process, he noticed that there were people from all over the world in this group. He hadn't noticed them since many had already been there prior to his getting there. There was a large group of about ten Asian men and women. One of them spoke enough Spanish to translate what was going on. He noticed a few Middle Eastern men who could easily appear to be born in Mexico, but Joaquin noticed that they spoke Arabic when they were together. Then there was a small group of about five people from Africa. When it was their turn, the language barrier made things difficult because they didn't understand, but when the armed men pointed their guns at them, they took the packages and were escorted by one of the men.

Everyone was quiet throughout the whole process until it was the turn of the group with children. It was as if the whole world could hear as that first child was taken from his parent. The mothers didn't want to let go of their children, but the armed men tore the children away from their parents and placed the children on the back of a truck. The children started holding each other and crying out for their mothers or parents. Fear and confusion was all over the children as they were tossed onto that truck. One mother tried running to her child, but was met by one of the armed men who hit her in the head with his gun. She rolled over in agony as the blood from her head started spilling. Her child jumped from the truck and came to her, trying to hold her, but was kicked in the side, which caused the child to fall back on the ground. The child was crying and holding his side as he was tossed back into the truck. The man then grabbed the mother by the arm and pulled her away. The parents called out to their children that everything would be okay, but in their minds, they had no idea if they would ever see their children again.

No noise or cheering came from the people as they got aboard the train. The armed men had forced people to move from two of the cars as it arrived, so that they could keep their packages close. Those people tried to fit into the other cars, and many had to sit on top and hang off the sides of the train. Joaquin decided that he would find a spot on top of the train so that he could feel the breeze on his face as the train moved.

As they were all loaded and the train's horn blasted, indicating that it was ready to leave, Flaco yelled out to them, "Thank you all for your cooperation, and we will see you all soon on the other side."

With that, they set off on the four-hour train ride that should put them close to the border near Nuevo Laredo. The whole ride there, it seemed as though no one said a word. Even the deafening sound of the train seemed very quiet, reflecting the mood of the travelers. The looks on the parents' faces showed their devastation as they only hoped they would see their children again.

They arrived in Nuevo Laredo five hours later as the train was running slower than expected. The group was quickly met by some other men who secretly had guns on them, and they were all told to gather nearby so that they could be given further instructions. Along with the packages they already had, they needed to take another package with them to the American side across the Rio Grande River. There, they would hand off what they were carrying, and then they would be free to go.

It seemed a little too simple to Joaquin, and if any of his experiences had taught him anything, it's that it's never as easy as it seems with these types of people. They prey on the less fortunate and those who have everything to lose and nothing to gain but freedom or the return of their children. He figured he needed to keep complying until his life was put into danger; then, he would find a way out. Hopefully, he could free the other people as well, but that he wasn't so sure was possible.

They were then escorted through this path that led away from the train tracks and into a brush area. There was a van parked in a clearing, and when they approached the van, one of the men whistled, and several other men came out of the van. The group of travelers were told to go single file and take the package given to them. After they received that package, they were pointed in the direction they needed to go. Following each other to the river, they were told to keep a fast pace since they had a deadline they needed to make.

The sun was directly above them, and it wasn't as humid as it had been during the first part of the trip. The heat was dryer, and Joaquin could feel the sun more, but it was tolerable. He simply kept moving, but kept an eye on all the men directing them. He knew that, if he needed to, he could easily take the men moving them. It would be easier now that they weren't in a large group, but in a single-file line. He was helping a few keep up the pace as they weren't used to running this much, and they were falling behind. He just kept with his own plan of waiting and hoping they kept to their word and let them go when they crossed over.

When they reached the river, a line of people were already in the water, trying to get across. The water level was higher than normal, and it was moving quickly, so it was more difficult for them to cross easily. Many people tried to plead with the men to not make them go because they couldn't swim, but they didn't care and told them to hold on to the person in front or behind them.

"*Vámonos, rápido.* Hurry up; you need to get across quickly," the men shouted. "If you want to see your kids or family, you get the fuck over there now!"

As Joaquin was pushing through the current, he was holding on to a lady, and that lady was holding on to another woman. The three of them slowly made their way across. It was about halfway through, where the river was the deepest, when one of the women lost her footing. She pulled the other woman down with her, and Joaquin was dragged down as well, but he was able to keep his footing. As he pulled the one he had ahold of up, she panicked and let go of the woman she had. The woman had panicked to the point that she climbed onto Joaquin, and he was having trouble staying up and keeping his footing. The one woman who was let go couldn't catch her footing and was swept by the current. Joaquin tried to reach for her, but the woman on him pulled him back, and he couldn't. This caused a few others to panic as well; some lost their footing and were picked up by the current and taken away. Joaquin could only look on as he would see people yell for help and then go under fighting the currents until they were no longer visible. He kept pushing forward, almost having to carry the woman holding on for dear life.

Once on the other side, he let the woman down, and he fell to his knees out of exhaustion. He was able to catch his breath after a moment of coughing from all the river water that he had drunk and inhaled into his lungs. They were then told to keep moving so that they could drop off their packages. Small groups at a time, since they were taking a while to cross the river, were escorted to the van waiting for them on the American side. After the majority of the people had made it over, they were taken to where another van was, and they each placed their packages into the van as a man was counting.

"Bueno a todos por su ayuda," one of the armed men standing there told them. Thank you all for your help. "As promised, that gentleman over there will be handing out your money for getting these packages over here."

"What about our children?" a mother asked with tears in her eyes because they could not see their children anywhere.

"Oh yes, the children. I almost forgot. Well, now that you are in America, this is our land, and it is not free to cross through here. If you want to see your children again, those of you that were given money, you must pay that other gentleman over there." He pointed with his gun to a man who was up on a hill, waving. "The bad part is that it costs money to bring your children over here, so you need to pay more to get them back. The only way to do that is to go back across the river and bring more packages. Once that is done three times, you should have enough money to pay the man up that hill. Of course, if you don't have any children, the money we give you now may or may not be enough. It all depends on how he feels today. Otherwise, you're free to get in that line to go back to Mexico." As he pointed with his gun again, there was a line of people at the bridge and walking across it, back into Mexico.

Joaquin knew it was too good to be true. They found a way to get their drugs and money across and not risk themselves doing it. It was too easy to target the parents with children as they would pretty much do anything to get their children back.

Joaquin decided he was not going to have any part in this, and he chose to walk back to the line leading over the bridge to Mexico. He figured there had to be other ways across, and he could do it easier without putting anyone else in danger. On his way to the bridge, he was so upset with himself because there was really nothing he could do to help those people. He looked back as he reached the bridge, and another line of people was crossing back to go and retrieve more packages. Joaquin wished he could've done more to help them in any way, but, knowing how these men work, any pushback would mean killing innocent men, women, and children.

He was walking across the bridge, lost in thought, when in the distance he thought he heard his name, but ignored it because no one should know him. Then he heard it again and again. Joaquin looked over in the direction it was coming from, but kept walking. He couldn't see who was calling his name, but he did see someone trying to push backwards in a line of people who were going to America. He kept trying to see who it was, but the crowd was covering them. He kept on walking as he didn't know who it was and didn't want to find out it was someone he didn't want to see.

Then he heard his name louder, and the way it was said was way too familiar. He didn't want to think of who that could be. When he heard his name again, his breathing stopped, and he couldn't believe who it could be. Joaquin was afraid to turn around and goose bumps covered his body as he remembered hearing that voice in his ear. This must be another dream he was having; he just had to wake up. His palms immediately became sweaty, and his heart started beating so fast.

As Joaquin slowly turned around, he was stopped by the most beautiful smile he'd ever seen. "Is that really you?" he heard her voice say.

Chapter 12

Happily Ever After?

The doors were slow and loud as the officer pushed a button and called through his radio what door they were at. "Main corridor," he said.

Each door took its time opening and closing as the metal rubbed and squealed until the doors stopped with a loud crash. Joaquin and the other men in red-and-orange uniforms were being escorted to their cells. The sound didn't bother them anymore as they had been around it long enough to have grown accustomed to it.

"Outer SHU corridor," the officer called.

Due to their statuses, the detainees had to be kept in a unit with two-man cells, rather than large, open dorms. That way, they could be easily controlled if anything were to go wrong.

"Inner SHU door." The radio sounded throughout the hall as its speaker crackled.

Joaquin had heard of a facility that had the red-and-orange inmates housed together in a dorm setting. One of the Mexican nationals was picking on a young kid from China. This had been going on for several days, and it was only getting worse. The young man from China was beginning to not want to eat or come off his bunk. There were about six other Chinese nationals in the dorm with him, and they hadn't said anything.

One day, an officer took notice that the young man was not eating and didn't want to be social with anyone. He questioned one of the other Chinese nationals who spoke English, and they told him what was going on. The officer was told that it was being taken care of and that it would be resolved soon.

The officer called to inform his commanding officer what was happening, and while he was on the phone, he noticed a Chinese man walk up to the Mexican man who was being a bully and tell him something in Chinese. The Mexican man didn't understand, so he just waved him off and told him to walk away and leave him alone. The Chinese man started to turn and walk away, but quickly turned back around and at the same time pulled a lock in a sock from his waistband and struck the Mexican man in the face with it. When it struck, it immediately opened up a large gash across his face. This prompted the other Chinese men to do the same as they all hit the other Mexican men who were associated with the one bullying their fellow Chinese.

This sparked a riot amongst the two factions, and the officer called for immediate assistance. He attempted to leave, but was met by other men in the room who held him back. The guard was not hurt, but was taken to the bathroom area and made to wait until it died down. Joaquin heard it took several hours to calm down the detainees and to clean up the blood that was splattered everywhere. Since then, the detainees do not have access to locks, and the men in red-and-orange uniforms are kept in two-man cells.

Joaquin was given a cell on the bottom floor due to his age. He managed to get a cell to himself since he was only there for two days. He didn't care either way; he just wanted to get these two days over so he could be free of these places. It had been too long since he didn't have to share a room or anything with someone. He was going to enjoy these two days.

"¡Ay, mi Dios! I can't believe it's you!" Cati grabbed Joaquin and held him tight, crying loudly. She was smiling and full of joy, hugging him and trying to get as close as she could to him.

Joaquin was in shock and couldn't even muster a word because he couldn't believe this was Cati standing in front of him. Confusion took over, and disbelief flooded his thoughts. He pushed her back slightly, trying to be sure this woman was actually Cati.

"How can this be?" he said very quietly, almost mumbling to himself. "I-I-I buried you and your f-f-family."

Cati's expression turned from joy to sadness at that point; she held Joaquin's hands and pulled him to sit on a bench. Cati had no idea that her family had been killed, and hearing it for the first time was like a sharp blade to her heart. Joaquin still had a very confused look on his face, but Cati just held his hands.

"After they took you away, my *tia* from my father's side came to help my mom because she was so distraught over what happened. My mom couldn't believe that her own brother was such a bad man and would do such things to hurt people. After about a week, men came to the house looking for you and said that you had escaped. I really thought I had lost you and that I would never see you again, but when I heard that you escaped, I was so happy, and I took off to go look for you. I always knew you wanted to come to America, so I went off to try and find you. They must have come back to look for you, and when they saw me gone, they killed my family. Those *pinche cabrones*! I'll fucking kill them all!"

Joaquin, still with no expression on his face, finally let what Cati said set in. He just grabbed her and hugged her so tightly and didn't want to ever let her go again. He pulled back and kissed her as if he had never kissed her before and held her there until they had to gasp for air. They both had tears in their eyes and smiles finally were exchanged; they were together again.

"But that was almost more than three years ago that you would have left to find me, and you're just now getting here at the bridge?" Joaquin asked with a concerned look.

"*Mira*, Joaquin, this road is much more difficult for women than it is for men. If you only knew the things women have to endure to make it on this road. I was fortunate to make it here, especially because I was alone. Most women always travel with someone or in groups. Plus, I have only been sent back twice. I have a temporary visa that allows me to go back and forth to work now. I was here only to get medicine for the family I work for, then head back, but I found you instead."

Joaquin was still in a bit of shock and couldn't believe that, after all this time of thinking she was gone, Cati was actually sitting there with him. The tears kept pouring from his face as Cati was telling him about the family she worked for and how they were helping her find him. She also went on to tell him that they were helping her get her citizenship because she helped them so much; they didn't want to lose her.

"¿Y tú? How is it that you're coming from America and going back to Mexico?" Cati asked. "I thought you wanted to be in America."

"Well, I was trying to get to America, but the way I was trying was not the way I was hoping for. I decided to come back so I could find another way, but I found you instead." Joaquin then grabbed Cati and held her tight again, just to make sure she was actually real.

"So what do we do now? You just came back to Mexico, and I have my visa to get back to America. There are ways to get back, but that might take a little time. I have to get back to my job."

Joaquin told her, "It's quite all right. I think I can probably get over there without any problems. You run ahead, and I will catch up. I just need to find an easy way over there."

"What do you mean? There are guards everywhere, and if you get caught, you could go to jail. Then they'll send you back to Honduras. I don't want that to happen to you."

Cati's voice started rising, and Joaquin could tell that she did not like his idea. He simply kissed her again until she calmed down. When he felt her release the tension in her arms, he pulled away. "There, now trust me; everything will be fine. Just go through like normal, and I promise I shouldn't be but thirty minutes behind you," Joaquin said with a grin.

"Okay, but you better not leave me again, *cabrón*!" Cati told him as she made her way towards the line again.

When she turned to see Joaquin, he was already gone; she scanned the whole area, but didn't see him anywhere. She called out to him a couple of times, but when he didn't answer, she was forced to continue on in the line. Cati was filled with joy, knowing that she had found Joaquin and that they would be together. She had almost lost hope that they would ever be together again and had cried almost every night, praying to see him.

As Cati moved slowly towards the gate with all the other people patiently trying to get through, she couldn't help but think about her family and what would have happened to her if she hadn't left to look for Joaquin. Sadness came over her again at the thought of her never being able to see her parents again.

A slight bit of commotion at the gate broke her train of thought. A family was denied entry because they had an expired visa. The father of the family was furious because he claimed he was told he would still be able to go back and forth as they waited for the updated visa to arrive. This caused others in line to get upset as they had slowed the lines down, and some were begging on the family's behalf to just allow them through. The crowd quieted once they saw the family step to the side and be escorted by officers to an office by the gate. The line started moving again, with a few making remarks about how they felt mistreated just because they wanted to work and do better for their families. Others just stayed quiet and tried to keep to themselves.

"*Próximo en la fila.* Next in line, please," an officer yelled out.

Cati was next in line; she looked around again to see if she could see Joaquin, but she could not. She did see a few others stare at her for not moving to the desk, and she took the looks as a hint and went to where the officer was checking IDs and visas. Cati was feeling a little anxious because she didn't know what Joaquin was going to do and how he would get over the border to meet her. She took her time in hopes of giving Joaquin the added time he might need to cross, even though she had no idea what he had planned.

"State your business, please," the officer said, not even looking at Cati, only taking her visa and ID card.

"I need to go back to work. I had a little shopping to do, and now I must get back." Cati handed him the bag of medicine she purchased, along with some toys she bought for the family's children and some spices she liked from Mexico.

The officer, still not even looking at Cati, handed her back the IDs, and, while breathing a long sigh out, said, "Welcome to *los Estados Unidos*; have a safe trip." He was very monotone, and Cati could tell he really didn't want to be there. She had seen this officer before, and he usually had the longer lines because he really didn't check documents very well. So many people waited to be in his line.

As she collected her things, Cati continued to look back and around to see if she could spot Joaquin. Sadness had started to find its way in again as she passed the gate and Joaquin was not with her. She began thinking about what she was going to do because he did say that he would be thirty minutes behind her, but it took much longer than that to get through that long line. She only hoped that he wasn't picked up and taken before getting through the gate.

When she had crossed the last gate where a guard was standing, on his radio she heard something was happening close-by. That sparked several officers to run and head in that direction. This worried Cati because Joaquin was going to attempt to come over, and she felt the officers could be going after Joaquin. She started to run in that direction as well, hoping to see if this was about Joaquin. As she passed a large pillar, a hand reached out and pulled her back. She let out a scream, but quickly stopped when she realized it was Joaquin.

"Hey, where are you going? I'm not over there," he said as she punched him in the arm.

"*¡Me asustaste, cabrón!* Why would you do that?" she said with a large grin on her face, so relieved it was Joaquin.

"Wait a sec, how did you…?" Cati, with a puzzled face, looked back at the gate and then at Joaquin, then towards where the guards were headed.

"No time, let's go," Joaquin said as he pulled her away from the building.

The noise from the commotion began to fade the farther away they got from the border gate. They walked together, moving as quickly as they could without drawing any attention to themselves, until they were far enough away from the border. The city was pretty heavily populated as it was one of the main ports of entry for trade goods, and they were easily able to blend in and not seem out of place.

Cati already knew her way around the city as she lived there, so she escorted Joaquin to where she was staying. It was a small efficiency apartment behind the main house where she worked. She was paid a small salary and given room and board for her services. She helped the family she worked for with cooking, cleaning, and babysitting the two younger children. Both the husband and wife worked for the city and had very good jobs, but needed help in their home to look after the children and house duties. Cati was a "godsend," as the wife put it, because she could trust Cati with anything, and she would always be there to help and take care of anything they needed.

When they arrived at her employers' home, Joaquin stayed outside while Cati went in and told them the great news. Joaquin was amazed with the home as it was the largest he had ever seen for a single family. The grass was nice and green, and the bushes stood really tall along both sides of the yard. As he was admiring the house, Cati came outside very excited and followed by her employers.

"Hello, Joaquin, we've heard so much about you. *Me llamo* Franklin de la Cruz, and this is my wife, Sylvia." Franklin put his hand out and shook Joaquin's hand.

Joaquin felt the firm yet inviting grip Franklin gave and returned the same.

Sylvia was very happy, and she swatted Joaquin's hand away when he offered to shake her hand. "I don't shake hands, dear; I'm a hugger. Plus, if you're family to Cati, then you're family to us."

"*Mucho gusto.* Very nice to meet you both," Joaquin told them as he broke the tight hug from Sylvia. "I'm not entirely sure what Cati has told you about me, but I hope it was all good things," Joaquin said as he laughed.

That evening during supper, Joaquin and Franklin were talking, and Franklin asked, "So, Joaquin, I have to say, we almost didn't think we'd be able to find you. You are one difficult man to track." He chuckled.

"I am terribly sorry, Mr. Franklin. I have to admit that if I had known Cati was alive, I would've come looking for her sooner," Joaquin said. "I thought she died three years ago, and I was devastated. I didn't have any reason to come to America anymore, until recently."

"Why is that? What did finally bring you to America?" Sylvia asked from the other room as she was preparing to serve some *pastel* and *cafecito*.

"Well, initially my mother made me promise that I would find my way here and look for a beautiful woman to have a family with. I found my beautiful woman, but she was taken from me, so I thought, and my desire to come here fell away. I tried to stay in Mexico and make a living, but things were just too bad over there. I didn't want to get caught up in either being a good man and poor with no work, or joining the drug cartels and killing people. Those are not the only two choices I wanted, so I decided to take a chance, fulfill my mother's promise, and come to America."

Franklin was stunned at what Joaquin told him. "I had no idea it was that bad over there and that those were the only two choices you had."

"You no longer have anything to worry about," Sylvia said as she walked in with the coffee. "Both of you now have each other, and we are going to help you be together here in America. Don't you worry about a thing; we will make the right calls and make sure you have everything taken care of."

That made Joaquin and Cati happy. She hugged him so tight, and he felt as if he were on top of the world.

"All right, Joaquin, so what can you do for work?" Franklin asked after many of the conversations had died down. "We gotta find something for you so that you can raise your family. I mean, so long as you plan on having one, right?" he said with a grin and nudged Joaquin with his elbow.

"Oh, thank you so much, Mr. Franklin. I really appreciate it. Yes, I will need to find work," Joaquin said, looking at Cati. "We just need to get married before we talk about raising a family."

"Well, what are you waiting for? You better snag her up before someone else does!" Sylvia yelled very excitedly.

Joaquin then looked at Cati, and he was at a loss for words; he really didn't know what to say. He stood up as she was sitting after returning from the kitchen. At that moment, he wasn't sure what to do or actually say. He held one of her hands softly as he began to think. Finally, he said the first thing that came to his mind and tried to make it sound as romantic as possible. *"¿Pues, mi vida, vamos a hacer esto o qué?"* Are we going to do this or what? Joaquin's face was red as that wasn't how he had intended to propose, but that is all that would actually come out.

Everyone let out a laugh as Cati pulled him close to her and kissed him. "It's about time you asked me! I've waited years to hear you ask," she said with tears in her eyes and kissed him again.

The next morning, Joaquin got into Franklin's truck, and they headed out of town. "Okay, Joaquin, we're going for a little ride to go see a good friend of mine. His name is Alberto, but we call him Beto. He owns a welding shop just outside of Laredo, and he is always looking for guys to help. It probably won't be much to start, but if it's something you like and can get good at, you can make a pretty good living doing it."

Joaquin nodded his head, and they were pretty quiet for most of the ride.

"Thank you so much, Mr. Franklin. I can't even begin to tell you how much it means to me that you and your family have taken care of Cati and that you are willing to help us."

"Don't mention it, buddy. Cati is the best thing that has happened to our family, and she takes care of our kids so well. Plus, she wouldn't stop telling us how amazing you were and how quickly you learned the duties of her father's ranch. If a man can keep her talking that much, you must be a good man," Franklin told him, smiling.

After about forty-five minutes of driving, they came to a small town. It was nowhere near the size of Laredo, and it almost reminded Joaquin of some of the towns in Mexico. It seemed as though it was growing due to the oil rigs that were being built. There was a small general store off the main road, and when they turned down one of the side roads, he noticed a tire shop. It seemed odd to have a tire shop in the middle of the homes, but Joaquin didn't question it. He still didn't know how many things were here in America, so he just didn't bother questioning it.

Upon arriving at Franklin's friend's home—it was a couple of blocks down from the tire shop—he was already outside waiting for them. He was a small-statured man in a long-sleeved shirt. His jeans were neatly pressed, and he had on glasses. When they exited the truck, he walked up to Franklin and gave him a big handshake.

"Well, there goes the neighborhood," Beto yelled with a big smile on his face.

Joaquin came around the truck to join the two men, and Beto turned and put his hand out to him.

"Joaquin, this is my good friend Beto. He is a very quiet man, but don't let that fool you. He knows his stuff."

Joaquin took Beto's outstretched hand and noticed how firm his handshake was, especially for someone his size. Joaquin figured all that welding must have developed that strong grip.

"*Mucho gusto en conocerte,*" Joaquin replied.

"So, Franklin tells me you need some work? I can really use a good man that's willing to learn and work hard."

"*Sí, señor,* I am a quick learner, and I am willing to work as hard as it takes to learn everything."

"*Ándale,* that's what I want to hear," Beto said as he shook Joaquin's hand again and patted him on the shoulder.

Just as they were speaking, Beto's daughter came running across the street yelling, "It wasn't me. I didn't do it!" She ran right past the men standing there.

When Beto looked back from where she was running, he noticed smoke coming from an abandoned building. The three men ran to the building, and before they reached it, the fire had grown. It was too much for them to handle, and they had to get back because the heat was overwhelming.

It didn't take long for a fire truck to arrive and put out the fire. The fire marshal blamed some nearby kids playing with matches and asked if anyone had seen any children playing by the building. No one except Beto had seen anyone, but he wasn't going to tell on his daughter.

"I'm sorry for the commotion, guys. As you can see, I am going to have to have a talk with my daughter later this evening. Come by in a couple of days, Joaquin, and we will get started on what I need you to do."

Franklin and Joaquin shook his hand again and thanked him for the opportunity.

Two days later, Joaquin was working with Beto, and he was going over many of the duties. Joaquin was trying to hear everything Beto was saying, but he was a soft-spoken man, and Joaquin didn't want to keep asking him to repeat himself. Plus, it was difficult to hear with the drumming going on.

"*¿Qué es eso?* What is going on with all that drumming?" Joaquin asked.

"Oh, those are *los indios* that come and have their ceremonies here. They come from all over to do their rituals and most importantly the peyote. We have a *tia* in the family that collects and prepares the peyote for them. Even though she isn't a native, they respect her and treat her as one of their own. She is the only civilian given permission to grow and harvest peyote that isn't a native."

Joaquin was taken by the sounds of the drums, and they were close enough he could hear the singing and all the loud chants. He had never heard anything like that before, and it was so moving for him. He could listen all day, and it wouldn't bother him at all. There was something soothing and relaxing about the singing and drumming that spoke to Joaquin, and he felt the cries as each drum was hit.

Before leaving for the day, Joaquin went to say good-bye to Beto, and he noticed him talking with a family. They clearly had been walking a long time and possibly had just crossed the border because they were carrying bags, were all dirty, and appeared as though they hadn't bathed in a long time. As they left, Beto gave them jugs of water and some food from a fridge he had outside in his shop. He also gave them whatever cash he had in his pocket. They thanked him and walked off.

"We get people from across the border through here all the time. Mostly families with children. I try and help when I can and point them in the right direction. If no one helps those in need, then how can we expect others to help us when we need it?"

That day, Joaquin went home feeling different after learning about Beto's *tia* and the natives who came to the area. Then, seeing Beto's selfless act with that family. *It is good to know that there are people in this world like him,* Joaquin thought. He caught a ride with a group of men who his way every day to work some fields. They didn't mind stopping and taking Joaquin along for the ride. After they dropped him off at a gas station, Joaquin walked the rest of the way to Cati's small apartment.

When he arrived, the house seemed unusually quiet, especially for that time of day. He took the path to the apartment in the back and noticed a few men in suits standing in the living room of the main house. Joaquin didn't really think of anything unusual because he knew they worked for the city, so seeing people in suits around the house was normal. He was getting ready for a bath when Cati came running in with tears in her eyes.

"Tell me it's not true, Joaquin! Please tell me you didn't do what they say you did!" Cati said as she grabbed Joaquin by the shoulders and shook him.

Joaquin was caught off guard and unsure of what she was talking about. "Cati, *mi vida*, what are you talking about?"

"They say you did it!" Cati said.

Just then, the men in suits came in and went after Joaquin. "Joaquin Navarez, you are under arrest for the murders of two men at the airport in Arizona. You have the right to remain silent, anything you say can and will be used against you…" They continued to read Joaquin his Miranda rights, and he didn't even put up a fight.

Cati was there, along with Franklin and Sylvia. He just looked at Cati. She had tears flowing from her eyes, and she was still saying, "Please, Joaquin, tell me you didn't do what they say you did." Franklin just looked at Joaquin with disappointment as he held his wife close.

The men grabbed Joaquin by both arms, and one officer put restraints on his wrists; they walked him outside to the front of the house. Joaquin was still confused as to what was happening, and he didn't know why he wasn't fighting his way out of the situation. He could have easily taken the two men and ran away.

It wasn't until he was put into the back seat of the vehicle that it clicked. That officer had said "airport in Arizona." That's where he saw someone kill those two men in that hangar. But how did they have his name, and why were they saying he did it?

When they closed the car door, he looked at Cati as she was standing there crying. He mouthed to her, "¡Yo no lo hice!" When he said that, she turned and ran back to her apartment. The officers got into the vehicle, and they drove off. Joaquin just kept looking for Cati as the house grew smaller and smaller.

Chapter 13

Home

"*¡Cuenta, señores!* It's count time!"

It was the midday count, right after lunch, and everyone had to stand outside their cells so that the officers could come by and do a physical count. Joaquin couldn't even remember how many times he'd had to do this over the years; by now, it was so monotonous. He stood there as he normally did, waiting for the officer to come around to him. Today's officer was new, and he'd already lost count twice. Joaquin rolled his eyes as he watched the young officer pace back and forth with his pen and notepad. As Joaquin was watching the officer count, he glanced at the man with the giant letter on his forehead and noticed that he was already returning the glance.

"I thought I told you not to be looking my way, fucking old man! You obviously have a hard time listening. Don't worry. I'll help you fix that. No problem, bitch ass motherfucker!"

Joaquin looked away slowly as if he hadn't heard the man.

"Yeah, *puto*, look away, little scary ass bitch!"

One of the man's friends tried to calm him down and told him, "Dude, he's just an old man; leave him alone. He isn't worth it, bro."

"Nah, bro, fuck that shit. He fucking keeps staring at me like he wants to fuck me or something. I ain't about that shit, homie. He gonna learn you can't be sizing fuckers up and not get handled."

Joaquin was not trying to cause any issues that would prevent him from leaving in two days. He simply ignored the threats and had no intention of entertaining that man. Joaquin just took his attitude as ignorance; he probably hadn't been locked up before. Most men knew that you didn't mess around with the older inmates as they'd done their time and should be treated with respect. Younger guys who were new to the system always came in thinking that they could bully and push anyone around, until they were checked by someone bigger or by someone in authority.

Joaquin wasn't anyone in authority, nor did he force respect from anyone. He mainly kept to himself and over the years was able to gain the respect of all those in his units; no one bothered him.

That evening, Joaquin decided he needed to take a shower before sleep. He made his way to the shower area and began taking his shower. He was thinking about how he might find a place in Honduras near where he was born and maybe start a garden and grow beautiful flowers.

His thoughts were interrupted when he saw that man with the giant letter and two of his friends standing in the doorway. There was no escaping. Joaquin knew he might be able to take one of them, but not all three. He wasn't as young as he used to be, but if this was the way he was going to go, he at least wanted to take someone with him.

"What now, bitch ass mothafucka! Why do you keep staring at me like you want me, you fucking *puto*? I am not one you want to fuck with, and anyone on the outside can tell you that. If you have a problem with me, bitch, you best be ready to fix it because I don't quit or back down from no one!"

Joaquin was standing there naked, still rinsing himself off. He slowly turned off the water and reached for his towel. He began drying himself off as if he were not paying any attention to the men in the doorway.

"Hey, bitch! Did you hear what I just said? I don't give two shits how old you are. You disrespect me, and I'm going to fuck you up!" the man said.

"Yeah, I heard you, but what do you expect an old man like me to do?" Joaquin said as he turned to them.

One of the men's eyes grew wide, and Joaquin could see fear come over him immediately. He grabbed his other two friends and whispered something into their ears. They all looked back at Joaquin and almost at the same time said, "Oh shit, I'm so sorry!" Then they quickly turned to leave. One of them slipped on the wet floor, but steadied himself and walked away.

Later that evening before lights-out, Joaquin was sitting at the table, reading a magazine by himself, and the man with the giant letter on his forehead came up slowly.

"Hey, pops, I just want to say I am really sorry. I was totally out of line, and if there's anything I can do for you, please let me know," the man said with sincerity in his voice.

Without moving, and only looking up at the man, Joaquin just shook his head no and went back to reading.

The man just continued to say he was sorry and walked away with his head down.

That's when Joaquin noticed other men looking at him and whispering amongst themselves.

Joaquin was sitting in a dark room with a small table and two other chairs across from him. The double-sided mirror to the right of him reflected the single-bulb light hanging above the table. He was still restrained at his wrists, but this time his hands were in front of him. His ankles were restrained, and the chain was hooked to the floor so he couldn't run off. One detective came into the room holding a cup of coffee, and another followed behind him.

"Well if it ain't my buddy Pancho!" It was the same officer from Arizona. He still had a cigarette hanging from his mouth, and he still had the same mustache. "You are one sneaky bastard, aren't you?" he asked Joaquin. "You had me going for a moment there, let me tell you. I actually had you once, and, like an idiot, I let you go. Well, in case you were wondering, I was able to catch Mr. Telemantes a week after I let you go. That's when they gave me your case. I didn't have much to go on, but somehow all your info showed up on my desk. It was crazy to me too, but I had a lead and, well, I got you now. I can see you're still a dumb motherfucker because you still stayed close to the border, even after I told you not to. Damn, I guess you people are hard of hearing too."

"You'll have to forgive Detective Flowers; he's a little passionate about his job, as you can see. My name is Detective Smith, and I see you've already met my partner. Well, I have to say, Mr. Navarez, this is a pretty open-and-shut case. We have two dead bodies with witnesses putting you at the scene and fingerprints all over the murder weapon. Unless you have something we can use in your favor, you're looking at spending the rest of your life in jail, without the possibility of parole. So, you might want to consider getting a lawyer before you even say anything."

Joaquin sat thinking about what was just said. There was no one in the area who could have been a witness, and he had his fingerprints removed as part of his training with the HDM. Detective Flowers said he received all of this information on his desk mysteriously, which means Joaquin was being set up, and there was no way for him to fight it.

Detective Flowers leaned over and said to his partner, "Why even bother telling him to get a lawyer? You know these people can't afford one anyway, plus he hasn't said much since he's gotten here. Chances are he don't even understand what the hell we're saying." He then looked over at Joaquin and said, "Ain't that right, Pancho?" Then he laughed and got up to walk out. "Let's go; we've wasted enough time on this wetback. I gotta go catch the game. Maybe we can get him sent to one of those prisons that grow food, so he can feel at home picking lettuce or watermelons and shit so he can eat."

Detective Smith stood up and they both walked out the door.

Joaquin wanted to hurt Detective Flowers for what he said, but he figured the detective was just an insecure man and needed to bully others to feel good about himself. *Those types of people will always have a visit from Karma,* Joaquin thought to himself as he sat there waiting.

Shortly after, an officer came in and escorted Joaquin to a desk where he was fingerprinted and booked until his court date. He was taken to a holding cell where he would wait until he was taken to the county jail. The cell was cold and had several other men waiting in it as well. Joaquin was the only one from south of the border; the others just stared at him as they closed the heavy steel bars behind him.

Joaquin stayed quiet. He heard the other men in the cell making little remarks amongst themselves while looking at him. Things like "fucking spick," "dirty wetback," or even "dumbass beaner." He just sat there, not responding or letting on that he understood them.

After two days Joaquin was under the impression that he was being sent to the county jail, but instead his court date was moved to the following morning. He was shocked because he didn't think things moved that quickly.

An officer came and called his name, "Joaquin Navarez, let's go; your lawyer is here to see you."

This confused Joaquin as he never asked for a lawyer. He reluctantly followed the officer because he wasn't sure what was going on, since this was a new country, and he wasn't sure how the process worked here. Joaquin was escorted to a smaller room than the interrogation room he had been in. This room didn't have a two-sided mirror, and it was well lit.

When he entered, there was a man sitting at the table already; he had a beat-up briefcase, and papers were all over the place. The man had on a short-sleeved, button-down shirt that appeared a few sizes too small for him. The buttons seemed to be struggling to hold on as his stomach was pushing very hard, trying to be free. He had coffee stains on his chest and a pipe hanging from his mouth. His salt-and-pepper beard was too long to be a five-o'clock shadow.

"Mr. Navarez, please have a seat. I'm your court-appointed attorney, and I will be helping you with your case tomorrow morning. Do you have any questions at this time?" the attorney said loudly.

"Well, yes, I do have many questions," Joaquin responded.

"Oh, you do speak English; they told me you didn't speak it very well. Okay, that makes things a whole lot easier for me," the attorney stated. "Well, give me a few minutes while I finish the paperwork for my next case."

Joaquin just sat there as his attorney fumbled through all the paperwork on the table and signed a few things, then put all those papers away, took out a single sheet of paper, and placed it in front of Joaquin. He slid over a pen as Joaquin picked up the paper to look at it.

"What is this?" Joaquin asked.

"Oh, just the admission of guilt you gave to the two detectives the other day. I just need you to sign it here, initial here, and then sign at the very bottom. You do know how to sign your name, right?"

"What do you mean by 'my admission of guilt'? I didn't admit to anything. I didn't do anything that they say I did." Joaquin was beginning to get frustrated and very annoyed; he put the paper back down on the table and slid it back to the attorney.

The attorney let out a big sigh and adjusted himself in his seat. "Look, Mr. Navarez, I'm on your side here. I only want to help you, but with everything they have against you, your only way out of this is not to fight it and to admit you did what they said. You can fight it later with appeals, and they can really look into your case then. As for now, just sign the paperwork, and we can get you ready for what to expect tomorrow."

"I'm not signing anything because I know I didn't kill those men," Joaquin said as he sat back in his chair and crossed his arms.

"Have it your way; it's your funeral." The attorney took the paper and stuffed it back into his briefcase. He struggled to stand up, and it took him two tries before he could. He let out a loud groan, and his knees popped when he finally got up. He walked out partly hunched over and dragging his feet.

Joaquin was upset, but didn't want to explode, so he just tried to calm himself down. "*Pinche* lawyer didn't even give me his name or leave a card," Joaquin said as an officer came in to escort him back to the cell.

The following morning, Joaquin was escorted from his cell to a van that drove him to the courthouse. They entered through a back door used for inmates, and he was placed in a cell as he waited for his time in front of the judge.

Four hours later and after they had lunch, Joaquin was brought into the courtroom. There were a few people in the room, and he noticed Cati sitting there alone in the corner. She looked at him with tears in her eyes, and it nearly broke Joaquin. He'd just gotten her back, and now he was being taken away from her again. She held a handkerchief to her mouth as they brought him to the front and had him stand near a podium.

The judge was already sitting in his seat, arranging papers in front of him. "Who do we have here?" the judge asked.

"We have the State of Texas versus Joaquin Tejirina Navarez, Your Honor," an attorney with the prosecution stated. "We are charging Mr. Navarez with two counts of first-degree murder."

The judge reached out his hand; the bailiff took the papers from the attorney and gave it to the judge. He started looking over everything and shuffled them back and forth. He glanced at Joaquin a couple of times and then back at the papers. Joaquin just stood there expressionless.

"You want to explain to me why I'm having to deal with this if this happened in Arizona?" the judge asked in an irritated tone.

"Well, Your Honor, your friend Judge Jefferson asked if you could do him this favor as he was completely booked, and they wanted to get this over and done with."

The judge rolled his eyes and looked back at the paperwork. "Why aren't we doing this with a jury present? He doesn't even have his attorney here," the judge asked.

"Your Honor, if you look in the back of the file, you'll see a signed confession by Mr. Navarez, admitting to the crimes against him. He also asked that no attorney be present since he was admitting to these charges."

Joaquin glanced quickly over at the prosecuting attorney and couldn't believe what he was hearing. He glanced back at Cati, and she was crying; she stood up and walked out.

"This is not true. I didn't do anything!" Joaquin shouted.

"If you don't stay quiet, you will be removed," the judge yelled back at Joaquin. The officer standing next to Joaquin grabbed him firmly by the arm and told him to be quiet.

"I don't understand how this is happening. I didn't kill those men, and I didn't sign anything admitting this!" Joaquin tried to shake off the officer who had him by the arm.

"Get him outta here, bailiffs. I will not have this kind of disrespect in my courtroom." As they forcefully escorted Joaquin out of the room, the judge stated, "Based on your total disrespect for me and this courtroom and all the evidence provided against you, I find you guilty of all charges. Since you chose not to have your attorney present, you will not have the option to appeal. I sentence you to life in prison without the possibility of parole. Get him outta my sight!" The judge slammed his gavel down and didn't even look up as Joaquin was taken out of the room.

As they were leaving the courthouse, Joaquin saw Cati walking down the street, holding her arms close to each other and her head down. He wished he could hold her and kiss her. When they passed her, she looked up, they locked eyes for a moment, and he saw her mouth move to say "I love you!"

The officers continued on to the county jail, from where Joaquin would be transferred to the state prison. Pulling up to the prison, Joaquin felt a dark cloud hovering over the building, despite the bright and sunny day. There was some type of heavy feeling of evil as they approached the main gate. The officers checking the van with their mirror on wheels and verifying the paperwork seemed like a dream to Joaquin. He still couldn't believe that this happened and how quickly they did all of this without his knowledge. They were waved through and the large gate closed behind them as Joaquin would say good-bye to the world for the last time.

Everything seemed muzzled, and Joaquin couldn't hear anything or anyone speaking to him because he could only think of Cati and how he would never be able to hold her again. He went through the entire intake process very stoically, not paying any attention to what was being said or done to him. They had to force him to remove his clothing because he was just standing there, not moving or saying anything. He was given his fresh uniforms and bedding and escorted to his cell. As he was walking, he ignored and drowned out the sounds the other men were making as he walked past them. Some would spit at him, and others threw things at him.

"You're gonna be my bitch tonight!"

"Fresh meat, boys!"

"Look at him; he's already scared shitless!"

"That's right, sweetie, don't worry; I'll take good care of you later!"

Those remarks didn't even faze Joaquin as he walked to his cell. Once at his cell, the officer called on his radio to open the cell door. The door made a couple of rattling noises, but then it opened up, and Joaquin was told to walk through the opening in the bars. The officer pulled the door shut after Joaquin walked in.

There was already another man in there, and he seemed happy to see him. "*Hola, amigo, me llamo* Rudy," he told Joaquin. "Do you prefer the top or the bottom bunk? It doesn't matter to me; that's why I'm asking."

"*Hola*, I'm Joaquin," he replied.

"*Bueno, amigo*, I'm happy you're here. My English isn't very good, and it's nice to have a cellie that can speak Spanish. My last cellie was a *güerito*, and we didn't speak much. They usually try to keep us all segregated so that it seems more humane to put us with our own kind, but this new warden didn't like that. *Pues*, if you don't mind, I'll take the top bunk. I mean, if you're all right with that?"

"That's fine," Joaquin said, still not really wanting to engage in conversation.

"*¿De dónde eres? Yo soy de México.*"

"I'm from Honduras," Joaquin responded.

"That's cool, bro, *aquí* we're all just wetbacks and beaners to them. There's only the whites, blacks, chinos, and us. It'll be okay though, there's a lot of us here, and we stick together," Rudy told him.

Joaquin just nodded his head and lay on his bed without putting the covers on it. He just wanted to stay there quietly and hoped that if he closed his eyes and opened them, his sentence would be over, he could leave, and Cati would be there waiting for him. He'd never thought about ending his life, but if ever there was a time to think about it, now would be that time. Many thoughts kept going through his mind, and despite most of the thoughts being bad, he always came back to thinking about Cati and her smile.

The following morning, Rudy and Joaquin made their way to the chow hall. Rudy took the time to explain everything to Joaquin. The count times and what to do during that time. He explained the process for going outside and for getting reading materials. Phone call hours and shower times for their block. When they made it to the chow hall, they both grabbed their plates, and Rudy showed him where they always sat. As they were walking up to the tables, Rudy pointed out a man who was sitting surrounded by others.

"That's El Negro. He's like our *jefe* around here. He pretty much runs things for the *Mexicanos*. No one talks to him unless he wants you to talk to him. This is where we always sit and keep an eye on things. Hey, fuckers, this is Joaquin. He just came in last night," Rudy told the group of men at the table as he and Joaquin sat down.

The men just mumbled, and a few ignored Rudy. A couple of the guys nodded or gave a "what's up" by flipping their head back quickly.

They ate their food before going out for recreation time. Joaquin learned that Rudy was in there for robbing a store and assaulting an officer. They gave him ten years because he punched the officer in the jaw and broke it.

"Fuck that officer; he called my mom a dirty wetback. I wasn't even trying to rob the place. That store owner ripped off my mom because she cashes her checks there. I showed up with my gun, and this fool has the nerve to call the cops on me. Then, when I try and explain this to that *puto* cop, he says he doesn't care about me or my dirty wetback mom. I was like, 'ain't this about a bitch!' So when that *puto* tried to put his hands on me, I swung and hit that *culero* in the jaw. He fell like a bag of beans!" Rudy started laughing and clapped his hands. "But, hey, no worries, *ese*, we already know why you're in here. Not sure why you did it, but I'm sure you had your reasons. We all have our reasons for doing what we did to wind up locked up in this shit hole."

An officer came up to Joaquin and called out his number, "N2306, you have a visitor."

This caught Joaquin off guard because he had no reason to expect any visitor. He got up from his seat and walked with the officer. There was a corridor that led to the visitation room, and the officer led Joaquin through that door. Along the wall, there were several seats that had dividers between them. Each seat had a telephone, and Joaquin was instructed to sit in the farthest one from the door.

When he reached the seat, he saw Cati sitting there with the saddest smile he had ever seen. Her face was shiny from all the dried tears. There was a big glass window separating them. As he sat, Cati and Joaquin picked up their phones at almost at the same time.

"Cati, *mi vida!*"

Cati held up her hand and shook her head. "Please, let me say what I need to say, and then I'll let you be." She took a deep breath and fought back more tears as she began to speak. "I don't know if you did what they say you did. I don't know if you are the same man I fell in love with. What I do know is that everything they say you did, they're showing proof that it was you. What I also know is that if you did do it, I'm sure you had a good reason to do it. I don't know what you went through when my *tio* had you, but I can only imagine what you had to do to get away. The other thing I do know is, no matter what, I still, and will always, love you. You have never been *feo* with me, and you always show me how much you love me."

Joaquin had tears in his eyes after she finished what she was saying. She put her hand up to the glass window, and Joaquin did the same. He was thankful that she didn't hate him for what they said he did and that she still wanted to see him after all that. Flashes of all the good times they spent together flooded his mind, and he didn't want her to leave. He then thought about how he would spend the rest of his life in jail and how he didn't want her to waste her time with him.

"*Mi vida*, you are my life and the reason I went through hell to find you again. There is nothing I wouldn't do to be with you. Believe me when I tell you this; I did not kill those men. I have done many things in my life, but killing those men was not one of those. I don't know why they are trying to put this on me, but I promise you, with all of my life and being, it was not me." Joaquin began to get angry at the thought that he was wronged and there was nothing he could do to fix it. He hit the table with his fist really hard, making a loud thud.

"Hey, none of that, inmate, or your visit is over!" the officer watching him said.

"Sorry, Officer, it won't happen again," Joaquin turned and told him. He then turned back and told Cati, "*Mira*, Cati, I don't want you coming here looking for me. It's not that I don't want you; it's because this is no place for a woman to be coming. This is a very bad place, and I need you to move on past me and forget about me. I am not getting out again, and we will never be able to see each other past this *pinche* window. You are still young, and you need to find someone else that can make you happy."

This caused Cati to start crying more. "But I don't want to lose you again. I love you too much not to come see you," Cati told him.

"You can't love someone that will not be there for you. You have to leave and not come back. Just, please, do as I ask and not come back," Joaquin said in a stern tone. He then stood up, walked away, and told the guard he was ready to go back.

"Joaquin! Joaquin! Please don't leave me this way! I beg you!" Cati banged on the glass as he walked back through the door and down the corridor. She sat there crying for several minutes, hoping he would come back, but he never did. She left the prison feeling as if her heart had been ripped from her chest and smashed into a million pieces.

Joaquin was walking back to his cell when Rudy approached him. "Hey, *vato*, heard you had a visit from your old lady."

"She isn't my old lady, and she won't be coming back anymore," Joaquin said in a soft, saddened voice.

"Shit, it's for the best anyway, homie. This isn't any place you want your lady to see you," Rudy said. "*Pues*, anyway, El Negro wants to talk to you, so we gotta go."

"What does he want from me?" Joaquin asked. "I just got here."

"I don't know, *vato*, but when El Negro calls, you gotta answer; otherwise, you won't like how he calls the next time."

Joaquin agreed and followed Rudy up to the cells where El Negro was. There were a couple of men standing outside the cell as if they were security for El Negro. Rudy and Joaquin were stopped before they got to the cell.

"Hey, *pendejo*, El Negro called for us," Rudy said, pushing past the man in his way.

"I didn't call for you, *cabrón*. I called for Joaquin, *culero*. Take a hike," a voice from inside the cell called out.

Rudy stopped in his tracks, put his head down, and turned to walk away. As he walked past the man in his way, that man smacked Rudy on the head.

"Come on in, Joaquin. Don't worry; we don't bite," El Negro called out, and it drew chuckles from the men in the room and outside the door.

Joaquin walked in cautiously, but not scared. He saw three other men inside the cell. One, on top of the bunk with his legs hanging off to the side, was skinny and had tattoos all over his arms. His hair was combed back and held in place with a hairnet. Another, standing by the door against the wall, seemed fairly heavyset, but also muscular. He outweighed Joaquin by at least fifty pounds or more.

El Negro was lying down on the bottom bunk, with his hands behind his head and his legs crossed. When Joaquin walked in, he stood up and was not very tall, but he was stocky and took care of himself.

"You called for me? How can I help you?" Joaquin asked.

"Well, the question isn't how you can help me; it's more of how can I help you? You see, we here on this cellblock take care of each other, and we provide a service to all those that come here that are Mexicanos or of Latin culture. It really isn't any cost to you, but a small favor here and there when asked. This will make sure that you have anything you need and protection from the wolves that are out there. *¿Me entiendes?*"

"Thank you for offering your services, but I was not looking at getting involved in any gangs or clubs. I have a long time in here, and I just want to live in peace and keep to myself," Joaquin answered in the most respectful way he could.

"I can respect that, but what you don't understand is that if you're not with us, you don't have any protection, and anybody can come at you at will." El Negro looked at the guys behind Joaquin, and they grabbed him by the arms and held them out.

Joaquin wasn't sure if he should fight them off and risk getting killed the second day he was here, or just wait to see how this played out. He just stood there as El Negro walked up to him, pulled out a knife, and cut his shirt down the middle. Joaquin didn't flinch as the cold blade touched his skin a couple of times as it was cutting through Joaquin's white T-shirt and uniform top.

"It's simple, *vato*. If you don't want our services, you gotta wear the mark of rejection, and then everyone will know you had your chance to be a part of us but didn't want it. It'll just be a small X over your heart with this blade. You sure that's what you want?"

El Negro put the blade to the side of Joaquin's face and slowly moved it up and down as if he were shaving him. The men holding Joaquin pulled his shirt off and held him tightly as they knew this was going to hurt. El Negro was getting ready to put the mark on Joaquin, but stopped as he looked at his chest where the brand of the HDM was. He hesitated when he saw that brand, and a look of confusion swept his face.

"Everyone, get the fuck outta here," he told the men in the cell. "Except you, we need to talk about this mark on your chest," he told Joaquin, tapping it with the blade of the knife.

The other men started to leave, but stopped and looked back at El Negro.

"Did I stutter, *pendejos*? Get the fuck out, and I'll call you when I need you," he yelled at the men.

They left quickly.

El Negro sat down on his bed and invited Joaquin to sit in the chair by his desk.

Joaquin slowly sat down, not knowing what just happened and why El Negro wanted to be alone with him.

"Let me first start off with saying I am sorry for how we treated you, Señor Navarez. If I had known it was you, I would have approached you sooner and in a different manner. We are at your service, and anything you need is at your disposal."

"I told you. I don't want anything from you or need any of your services. I just want to be left alone and to live out my life here in peace," Joaquin said again.

"Very well, Señor Navarez. All will leave you alone, and you will not have to worry about anyone here bothering you. If there is anything I can do for you, please don't hesitate to ask." El Negro's tone and voice had changed, and he was being more submissive towards Joaquin. "Please, at least allow me to replace the shirts I tore." He reached under his mattress and pulled out a new T-shirt and a new uniform top and gave them to Joaquin.

"Thank you, jefe," Joaquin said while changing his shirts.

"No, no, sir, you call me El Negro if you like."

Joaquin turned and walked out of the room very confused. Just a few moments ago he was about to get another brand on his chest, and now he was walking out, unsure what happened. He walked back to his cell and Rudy was there waiting; he jumped up when he saw Joaquin.

"*¿Pues, que pasó, vato?* What the fuck happened? Did you take his protection, or did you take the X on your chest? If you took the X, I am going to have to put in a transfer out of this cell. I can't be associated with someone not under El Negro's protection. That's bad news for both of us, *ese*." Rudy seemed anxious to know what Joaquin chose and couldn't stop moving around.

"Relax, Rudy, *tranquilo*," Joaquin told Rudy. "I didn't need to do anything. I'm not a part of your *clica*, and I didn't need to get the X on my chest. We came to an understanding and have a mutual agreement."

"*¿Qué?* What the fuck do you mean, a mutual agreement? What is that?" Rudy asked, very confused.

"Listen, no need to worry, *mi amigo*, all will be fine, and hopefully they'll leave us alone," Joaquin said, smacking Rudy on the shoulder as he went to lie down.

Later that evening around dinnertime, they were called to eat. They exited their cell and began walking toward the chow hall. Things seemed very different in that cell block as everyone seemed to be focused on Joaquin and Rudy. They noticed others stopping, letting them pass, and then following behind them since they were all headed to the same place. Rudy took notice rather quickly since he had been there longer, and no one ever treated him that way before. At the chow hall when they got at the end of line to wait for their food, the men in the line in front of them all moved back behind Joaquin and Rudy.

"Okay, what the fuck is going on here? What the hell happened in that room that you are getting this treatment?" Rudy asked.

"I honestly don't know. Your guess is as good as mine," Joaquin replied.

They walked forward and grabbed a plate, and no one looked them in the eyes. The servers kept their heads down and handed them each a plate that had more food than the other inmates were getting. They then went to find a table. As they passed one, the men occupying it stood up and moved to another table, leaving theirs completely open for him and Rudy. Joaquin wasn't as hungry as Rudy, so he didn't finish everything on his plate. Rudy finished his plate and the rest of Joaquin's. For the first time since Rudy had been there, it was very quiet in the chow hall; they were all looking at Joaquin. After dinner, Joaquin decided he didn't want to go outside; rather, he just wanted to go lie down.

Rudy told him he'd catch him later, back in the cell. After about an hour, Rudy came back to the cell very quietly and didn't really say anything to Joaquin.

"Okay, let's hear it. What's going on out there, and why is everyone acting weird towards us?" Joaquin asked. Rudy didn't answer right away, so Joaquin stood up and looked at Rudy, who was lying on his bunk.

Rudy flinched and put his hands up. "I'm sorry, sir; please don't hurt me. I had no idea who you were, and now that everyone knows, you don't need to worry about anything," Rudy said with fear in his eyes.

"What are you talking about, *cabrón*? I am no one, and why are you acting like that with me?"

"Sir, they say you are the last remaining member of the most vicious cartel in all of Mexico. It's said that when you guys wanted to move in on another cartel, you made it look easy. That *placa* you have on your chest is what saved you. El Negro saw that and recognized it right away. His whole crew was destroyed by people that they called the

HDM or *Los Fantasmas*. You were feared because no one saw you coming, and they never saw you leave because they'd all be dead. So when he saw that *placa*, he thought you were here to finish him off, and he didn't want to die. He spread the word that you are not to be touched or bothered while you're here, and anyone breaking that will have to answer to them."

"Fuck!" Joaquin said, pissed off. "This is not what I wanted because, now that everyone knows who I am, someone is going to try and come after me to settle a score."

"Not going to happen, *ese*. You are protected, whether you like it or not. No one—I mean, no one—is going to bother you or your future cellmates. I really don't know what you are capable of doing, and, believe me, I don't want to be around to find out. If I am there, I just hope I'm not the one you're coming after."

A couple of weeks went by, and Joaquin was still trying to get used to everyone moving out of his way when he walked around. He mainly just stayed in his room and only went outside every couple of days. Even the guards gave him the same respect as the other inmates did.

"Señor Navarez, you have a visitor, sir," a guard told Joaquin as he was coming back from his shower.

Joaquin quickly got dressed and followed the officer to the visitation room. He was led to a different room this time. This visitation area had a few tables, and there was no glass separating them. Joaquin waked in and saw Cati sitting there, waiting with her arms crossed. She didn't have a smile on her face, but looked serious and sad.

Joaquin sat down in front of her, and they looked at each other, without saying a word, for what seemed like an eternity.

"I know you said you didn't want me to come see you, but I am tired of not being able to see you and people telling me what I can and cannot do. So I don't give a damn if you want to see me or not; I want to see you, and there's nothing you can say or do to change my mind."

Before Cati could get out another word, Joaquin reached over the table and gave her a kiss and a hug.

She pulled away, looking at the guards, who turned their attention somewhere else. She also noticed that another couple there saw them kiss; they tried to kiss each other too, but the guard stopped them.

"No touching; sit down, or your visit is over!" the guard told that couple.

They looked over at Joaquin and Cati, wondering why they couldn't touch, but Joaquin and Cati were allowed to hug and kiss.

Cati gave Joaquin a puzzled look, and Joaquin just shrugged his shoulders. They both chuckled and had a long conversation about how Cati was doing and how things were going for Joaquin inside.

"After your conviction, Sylvia and Franklin let me go because they couldn't be associated with someone convicted of murder, or especially have me around their children," Cati said and seemed really sad about losing her job. She had grown very close to the children and not being with them hurt the most. She told him that she moved closer to where he was so that she could come to visit him as often as possible. Cati told him she would put money into his account so he could buy things if he needed anything.

"There's no need to do that, *mi vida*. I have everything I need. Plus, with how they have things set up here in this place, we can have pretty much anything we ask for if we want it. I don't require much here, so you keep your money and make sure you're taken care of," Joaquin told her as he reached for her hand.

Cati had never heard of a prison that gave you anything you wanted, but didn't question it since Joaquin seemed okay and not lacking for anything. Their conversation continued, and they talked about anything that came to mind. When their time had ended, they hugged each other and kissed one more time. Cati waved as she walked away and told him she would see him next week. Joaquin was so happy and couldn't wait to see her again soon.

Over the next twenty years, Cati would come visit Joaquin every week, either on a Saturday or a Sunday. She never missed a week. Even when Joaquin was transferred to other facilities, Cati would find a way to be there to see him. They always took time to hug and kiss each other and talk about what life would be if Joaquin were on the outside, out of prison.

Despite how easy things had been for Joaquin, after moving from facility to facility, his reputation began to fade. He became just an older man doing his time. They just left him alone and didn't bother with him. That didn't trouble Joaquin at all since he just wanted to be left to himself anyway.

Cati's visits started slowing at about the twenty-third year, and Joaquin noticed a difference in her appearance. She aged dramatically, and she appeared to tire just from talking. He would ask her over and over if she was okay, but she would always say she was fine. Joaquin knew something was going on, but didn't want to push her if she didn't want to say. He noticed as she would leave that she walked very slowly and needed the help of one of the officers to walk out of the facility.

One year, she stopped showing up. Joaquin would wait week after week, hoping she would visit, but she never did. There was no way of reaching out because she had never given him an address or phone number to reach her if he needed to. She always came to visit, so there was no need to give him that information.

For six months, Joaquin kept hoping that she would show up. Finally, he stopped waiting and got used to the idea that she was no longer going to visit. One day, a letter came for him, and it was written by Cati. He was beyond excited to finally receive some indication that she was okay. He sat up quickly and tore the letter open like it was a gift on Christmas morning. Inside, there was a handwritten letter and a photo of Cati when she was younger. Joaquin looked at the picture and gave it a kiss, as if she were actually there, before reading the letter.

My dearest Joaquin,

I can't begin to tell you how sorry I am that I cannot be there with you to visit every week like I promised. There is nowhere else I'd rather be than spending time with you. With each week that passed that I didn't see you, it ripped a piece of my heart out. I looked forward to all the time we spent together, regardless of how short the time was. Getting a hug and kiss from you meant more than anything each week. I loved how we would talk about how our lives would be together if you weren't in that place and the family we could've had.

I'm sorry to tell you that you were right to ask if something was wrong with me. I didn't want to tell you because there was nothing you could do, and I didn't want to waste our time talking about me and what is wrong.

By the time this letter reaches you, I probably will have lost my fight to breast cancer, and I will be joining my family in heaven. You have meant the world to me and kept me going all these years. I only pray that one day we will see each other again, and we can live the happy life we always wanted.

Thank you for always looking out for me and for finding me.

I love you.

Tu Vida,

Cati

Joaquin was barely able to read this letter as it was the love of his life telling him that she was dying. He cried the most he had ever cried that evening and skipped eating for the next couple of days. One of his friends had to force him to get out of bed and eat something. Joaquin was devastated and heartbroken at the news from Cati. He tried to push it out of his mind, but the pain was just too great. It took him almost an entire year to cope with the idea that Cati was gone, and he would never see her again. The last memory he had of her was watching her struggle to walk out the door. If he had known that would be the last time he'd see her, he would've held on to her longer.

One day, a few years after Cati's death, Joaquin got a call from an officer. "Mr. Navarez, gather your things; you're outta here."

"Yes, sir, boss, right away," Joaquin told the officer. He figured he was being transferred again as it was his second transfer in two months. He was actually getting tired of moving back and forth. "Do you know where I'm going this time, boss?" he asked.

"I believe El Paso," the officer said.

"El Paso?" Joaquin asked. "What the hell am I going to do over there? Isn't that just a detention center?"

"Your guess is as good as mine. Just hurry up because you need to leave in like thirty minutes," the officer told him.

Joaquin quickly gathered his things, which only consisted of a few notepads and a couple of books on growing flowers. He liked to read books on how to grow the best flowers, hoping one day he might be able to do so. He also had the letter and photo that Cati sent him in the Bible he kept under his pillow; he would look at her picture every night.

He was put in a large van by himself, and the drive was about three hours from Pecos to El Paso. He had asked the officers why he was going to a detention facility in El Paso, but they couldn't answer and only said they were given orders to take him there.

Once he arrived in El Paso, he was taken to a room in which some immigration officers were sitting. He was instructed to have a seat; an officer would be with him shortly. Joaquin was starting to worry that something was wrong, and he wanted to know what all this was about. He began to get impatient when an officer called him over.

"Joaquin Navarez? Is that you?"

"*Sí*, that's me," Joaquin responded.

"Great, come have a seat over here, please," the officer instructed, and Joaquin complied without any restraint. "Let me first begin by saying I do apologize for all the moving around you had to do, then bringing you out here at the last minute, and no one being able to tell you what's going on."

"That's all right, Officer. I'm just very curious as to what is going on, is all," Joaquin told him.

"Well, we just recently discovered that a Detective Flowers had been convicted of tampering with evidence and doctoring paperwork to wrongfully convict individuals like yourself, just to make himself look like a super cop. This prompted all his cases to be looked at, and yours so happened to be one of his first ones throughout his long career. Well, I am pleased to tell you that you are going home. I do understand that being locked up for thirty years has been difficult, but I assure you that you no longer have to stay locked in a cage."

Joaquin couldn't believe what he was hearing. It all seemed unreal. He knew he had been wrongfully convicted, but there was no way someone with his status could prove it. He just prayed and hoped one day he would be set free.

"There's only one unfortunate matter we need to discuss, Mr. Navarez. Due to the fact that you are in this country illegally, if we release you from prison, you will need to be deported back to your country of origin. Can you confirm which country you are from? I have in my system you were born in Mexico."

The thought of being free was more than enough for Joaquin, but to be deported back to where he was born, now that was something he hadn't thought of. Either way, getting out of prison was the only thing he cared about, and if that meant sending him to Australia, he didn't care.

"I was born in Honduras," he told the officer.

"Well, that changes a few things, then." The officer typed away at his computer, writing up a report of what Joaquin told him. "You're in luck, Mr. Navarez; a plane leaves in a few days, but you have to fly out of San Antonio, and that means there's a holding facility you need to stay at until that plane leaves. You'll have to catch a ride on a bus that leaves tomorrow for that facility, so you'll just spend the night here and leave first thing in the morning. Normally, this process takes weeks, if not months, for someone to actually be taken back to their country of origin, but, given these circumstances, we speeded things up a little. Hope that is okay with you."

Joaquin nodded and had to let everything the officer told him sink in. It all seemed surreal to him after so many years.

Joaquin put his magazine down, walked back to his cell, and went to sleep. He could only imagine what the men were whispering about him, and he didn't care to know anymore. He only had one more day to go before he was sent home. That day couldn't come fast enough, and it was a day he had been looking forward to for a very long time.

"Okay, Mr. Joaquin T. Navarez, do you have your things packed and ready to go?" an officer asked him.

"Yes, sir, boss. I am ready to go." That form of address will always stick with those who have been in prison for a long period of time. "Yes, sir, boss."

Joaquin felt good about getting on the bus with all the other Honduran nationals headed to San Antonio to get on the airplane. It would be a five-hour flight, which seemed crazy when most of these men took weeks to get here on foot. Their spirits were lifted as most didn't mind going home, unlike others who knew that they needed to get back as soon as possible to the United States.

It all happened so quickly, the bus ride to the airport and then the flight back to Tegucigalpa. There, they were given all their personal belongings and bus fare to be taken as close to wherever they lived if they wanted. Joaquin had no real clue where he was actually from, so he just chose a town close-by.

The bus was full, and he had to stand for most of the ride. It wasn't an hour later a seat opened up, and then he was able to sit down. The bus finally came to a stop, and the bus driver yelled out the name of a town. This is where he needed to get off.

As Joaquin climbed down the old bus's steps, he was left on a dirt road. He looked around, and as the bus drove off, it left a bunch of dust in the air, causing him to cough. Once the bus was too far to hear, the road was quiet, and the only sounds Joaquin could hear was his own breathing and a couple of birds that flew by.

The bag of personal things he was given had a box that appeared to have been mailed. He looked it over and noticed it was from Cati; it was mailed the same day he received the letter from her. When he shook the box, Joaquin could hear something rolling around that seemed rigid. After opening the box, he reached in and pulled out his father's knife. A smile came over face, along with a tear, seeing that knife and knowing that Cati had kept it for him all this time.

Joaquin stood there, looking out over this land he had not seen in so many years and trying to remember any connection he might still have with it. So many tears shed, so many loved ones lost, and he was right back to where he started. He looked up the road in one direction and then turned to look in the other. One way was south, and the other was north. One way was his past, and the other should have been his future.

Joaquin let out a long sigh as he started walking. The sign he passed read, "*Estados Unidos* 2,600 km."